# JEOPARDY!™

## What Is Quiz Book 1?

# Other Books

*Jeopardy! . . . What Is Quiz Book 2?*

# JEOPARDY!

## What Is Quiz Book 1?

**Andrews McMeel
Publishing**

Kansas City

# JEOPARDY!™

## What Is Quiz Book 1?

# JEOPARDY!™

# 2-LETTER WORDS

| Clue | Value | Response |
|------|-------|----------|
| PEOPLE WITH A HIDDEN AGENDA OFTEN HAVE THIS "TO GRIND" | $100 | WHAT IS |
| "COLLECT $200" IF YOU CAN NAME THIS JAPANESE GAME PLAYED WITH BLACK & WHITE COUNTERS ON A CHECKERED BOARD | $200 | WHAT IS |
| AS A PREFIX, IT CAN MEAN "NOT INCLUD-ING"; BY ITSELF, IT MEANS "FORMER", LIKE A FORMER SPOUSE | $300 | WHAT IS |
| YES, IT'S RUSSIAN FOR YES | $400 | WHAT IS |
| "VERY", "WHAT'S YOUR POINT?" OR THE TITLE OF A PETER GABRIEL ALBUM | $500 | WHAT IS |

# JEOPARDY!

## 2-LETTER WORDS

| | |
|---|---|
| **$100** | WHAT IS AN AX? **$100** |
| **$200** | WHAT IS GO? **$200** |
| **$300** | WHAT IS EX? **$300** |
| **$400** | WHAT IS DA? **$400** |
| **$500** | WHAT IS SO? **$500** |

# JEOPARDY!

## KIDDY LIT

| | | |
|---|---|---|
| IT'S A PARROT, NAMED POLYNESIA, WHO TEACHES THIS DOCTOR THE LANGUAGE OF ANIMALS | $100 | WHO IS |
| THE FRONTISPIECE OF THIS ROBERT LOUIS STEVENSON PIRATE BOOK FEATURED A DETAILED MAP | $200 | WHAT IS |
| "THE GREAT SWANS SWAM ROUND HIM, STROKING HIM WELCOMINGLY" | $300 | WHO IS |
| HE WAS "BAWN AND BRED IN A BRIER-PATCH" | $400 | WHO IS |
| THIS BOOK BEGINS WITH THE MOLE "SPRING-CLEANING HIS LITTLE HOME" | $500 | WHAT IS |

# JEOPARDY!

## KIDDY LIT

$100  WHO IS DOCTOR (JOHN) DOLITTLE?  $100

$200  WHAT IS "TREASURE ISLAND"?  $200

$300  WHO IS THE UGLY DUCKLING?  $300

$400  WHO IS BRER RABBIT?  $400

$500  WHAT IS "THE WIND IN THE WILLOWS"?  $500

# JEOPARDY!

# ANIMALS ON THE MAP

| Clue | Value | Response |
|---|---|---|
| A 4,083-FOOT-HIGH VERMONT MOUNTAIN IS NAMED FOR THIS CAMEL FEATURE | **$100** | WHAT IS |
| LOCATED AT THE HEAD OF THE NIAGARA RIVER, IT'S THE SEAT OF NEW YORK'S ERIE COUNTY | **$200** | WHAT IS |
| "THE WORLD IS NOT ENOUGH" ENDS WITH JAMES BOND & A WOMAN NAMED CHRISTMAS IN THIS EUROPEAN-ASIAN COUNTRY | **$300** | WHAT IS |
| IN OTHER WORDS, THIS VACATION AREA IN CALIFORNIA'S SAN BERNARDINO MOUNTAINS WOULD BE "LARGE GRIZZLY" | **$400** | WHAT IS |
| THIS RIVER WINDS ITS WAY THROUGH HELLS CANYON | **$500** | WHAT IS |

5

# JEOPARDY!

# ANIMALS ON THE MAP

$100 · WHAT IS A (CAMEL'S) HUMP? · $100

$200 · WHAT IS BUFFALO? · $200

$300 · WHAT IS TURKEY? · $300

$400 · WHAT IS BIG BEAR (VALLEY)? (ACCEPT: BIG BEAR LAKE) · $400

$500 · WHAT IS THE SNAKE RIVER? · $500

# JEOPARDY!

## TRANSPORTATION

| | | |
|---|---|---|
| THIS ALLITERATIVE TERM FOR A CAR WITH LOW FUEL EFFICIENCY BECAME COMMON IN THE 1970S | **$100** | WHAT IS |
| FOUND ON MANY SPORT UTILITY VEHICLES, IT'S A SYSTEM WHERE BOTH AXLES PROVIDE PROPULSION | **$200** | WHAT IS |
| TRANSPORT THAT HELPED THE FINNS IN THE 1939-40 WINTER WAR & HELPED FINN MATTI NYKAENEN WIN OLYMPIC GOLD | **$300** | WHAT ARE |
| IT WAS CREATED IN 1971 & FORMALLY CALLED THE NATIONAL RAILROAD PASSENGER CORPORATION | **$400** | WHAT IS |
| THIS DEVICE INCREASES A JET PLANE'S THRUST BY BURNING EXHAUST GASES | **$500** | WHAT IS |

# JEOPARDY!

# TRANSPORTATION

| | | |
|---|---|---|
| **$100** | WHAT IS A GAS GUZZLER? | **$100** |
| **$200** | WHAT IS 4-WHEEL DRIVE? (ACCEPT: ALL-WHEEL DRIVE) | **$200** |
| **$300** | WHAT ARE SKIS? | **$300** |
| **$400** | WHAT IS AMTRAK? | **$400** |
| **$500** | WHAT IS AN AFTERBURNER? (ACCEPT: TAIL PIPE BURNER) | **$500** |

# JEOPARDY!

## PEOPLE IN SONG

| | | |
|---|---|---|
| JIM CROCE'S FIRST NO. 1 HIT WAS ABOUT THIS "BAD BAD" MAN | **$100** | WHO IS |
| IT'S WHOM THE McCOYS TOLD TO "HANG ON" IN 1965 | **$200** | WHO IS |
| ELTON JOHN HAD A 1975 HIT WITH THIS PSYCHEDELIC BEATLES SONG | **$300** | WHAT IS |
| SHE WAS "DIRTY" IN THE TITLE OF A SONG FROM MICHAEL JACKSON'S ALBUM "BAD" | **$400** | WHO IS |
| LOU REED'S SONG ABOUT THIS "SWEET" FEMALE APPEARS ON THE VELVET UNDERGROUND ALBUM "LOADED" | **$500** | WHO IS |

# JEOPARDY!

## PEOPLE IN SONG

**$100**  WHO IS (BAD BAD) LEROY BROWN?  **$100**

**$200**  WHO IS SLOOPY?  **$200**

**$300**  WHAT IS "LUCY IN THE SKY WITH DIAMONDS"?  **$300**

**$400**  WHO IS DIANA?  **$400**

**$500**  WHO IS "SWEET JANE"?  **$500**

# JEOPARDY!

## "LITTLE" WOMEN

| | | |
|---|---|---|
| NURSERY RHYME CONSUMER OF CURDS & WHEY | **$100** | WHO IS |
| ONCE CAROLE KING'S BABYSITTER, SHE URGED US TO "DO THE LOCO-MOTION" | **$200** | WHO IS |
| THIS H.C. ANDERSEN CHARACTER TRIES TO KEEP WARM ON NEW YEAR'S EVE & HAS VISIONS OF HER GRANDMOTHER | **$300** | WHO IS |
| THIS MISCHIEVOUS GIRL WITH CORKSCREW CURLS APPEARED IN THE SATURDAY EVENING POST FOR OVER 10 YEARS | **$400** | WHO IS |
| THIS FRANCES HODGSON BURNETT TITLE CHARACTER IS NOT THE FEMALE VERSION OF A SAINT-EXUPERY CHARACTER | **$500** | WHO IS |

# JEOPARDY!™

## "LITTLE" WOMEN

**$100** — WHO IS LITTLE MISS MUFFET? — **$100**

**$200** — WHO IS LITTLE EVA? — **$200**

**$300** — WHO IS THE LITTLE MATCH GIRL? — **$300**

**$400** — WHO IS LITTLE LULU? — **$400**

**$500** — WHO IS "A LITTLE PRINCESS"? — **$500**

# DOUBLE JEOPARDY!

## EUROPEAN PAINTERS

| | | |
|---|---|---|
| THIS PORTRAYER OF PARISIAN NIGHTLIFE WAS DESCENDED FROM THE COUNTS OF TOULOUSE | **$200** | WHO IS |
| HE COMPLETED HIS PAINTINGS OF "MORN-INGS ON THE SEINE" BEFORE BEGINNING HIS "WATER LILIES" | **$400** | WHO IS |
| AROUND 1485 THIS FLORENTINE PAINTED "MARS AND VENUS" & "THE BIRTH OF VENUS" | **$600** | WHO IS |
| YOU MIGHT "SCREAM" WHEN YOU SEE THIS NORWEGIAN'S "SELF-PORTRAIT WITH SKELETON ARM" | **$800** | WHO IS |
| THIS SPANIARD WAS NAMED FIRST COURT PAINTER TO KING CHARLES IV IN 1799 | **$1000** | WHO IS |

# DOUBLE JEOPARDY!

## EUROPEAN PAINTERS

$200    WHO IS HENRI DE TOULOUSE-LAUTREC?    $200

$400    WHO IS CLAUDE MONET?    $400

$600    WHO IS SANDRO BOTTICELLI?    $600

$800    WHO IS EDVARD MUNCH?    $800

$1000    WHO IS FRANCISCO GOYA?    $1000

# DOUBLE JEOPARDY!

## FUN & GAMES

| | | |
|---|---|---|
| THE "CHINESE" FORM OF THIS USES MARBLES RATHER THAN DISKS | **$200** | WHAT IS |
| "SHARE A SMILE" BECKY, BARBIE'S FIRST FRIEND WITH A DISABILITY, CAME COMPLETE WITH A PINK ONE OF THESE VEHICLES | **$400** | WHAT IS |
| INTRODUCED IN THE 1950s, THIS "MODELING COMPOUND" BEGAN AS A CLEANING PRODUCT FOR WALLPAPER | **$600** | WHAT IS |
| THE SECOND HALF OF A SYNONYM FOR TABLE TENNIS, OR THE FIRST SUCCESSFUL VIDEO GAME | **$800** | WHAT IS |
| JOHNNY CARSON & EVA GABOR MADE THIS PARTY GAME A HIT WHEN THEY TRIED IT ON TV | **$1000** | WHAT IS |

# DOUBLE JEOPARDY!

## FUN & GAMES

$200    WHAT IS CHECKERS?    $200

$400    WHAT IS A WHEELCHAIR?    $400

$600    WHAT IS PLAY-DOH?    $600

$800    WHAT IS PONG?    $800

$1000    WHAT IS TWISTER?    $1000

# DOUBLE JEOPARDY!

## CLASSIC FOREIGN FILMS

| | | |
|---|---|---|
| THE UNCUT VERSION OF THIS RUSSIAN EPIC BASED ON A TOLSTOY NOVEL IS MORE THAN 8 HOURS LONG | **$200** | WHAT IS |
| THIS FILM ALSO KNOWN AS "LES PARAPLUIES DE CHERBOURG" IS THE PERFECT RENTAL FOR A RAINY DAY | **$400** | WHAT IS |
| WHEN HE WAS LIVING IN ITALY, RICHARD SIMMONS APPEARED IN THE FOOD ORGY SCENE OF THIS DIRECTOR'S FILM "SATYRICON" | **$600** | WHO IS |
| TOSHIRO MIFUNE STARRED IN THIS DIRECTOR'S EPIC "THRONE OF BLOOD", SORT OF A SAMURAI VERSION OF "MACBETH" | **$800** | WHO IS |
| "SOLDIER OF ORANGE", A 1977 FILM FROM THIS COUNTRY, MADE RUTGER HAUER AN INTERNATIONAL STAR | **$1000** | WHAT IS |

# DOUBLE JEOPARDY!

## CLASSIC FOREIGN FILMS

| $200 | WHAT IS "WAR AND PEACE"? (ACCEPT: VOYNA I MIR) | $200 |
|---|---|---|
| $400 | WHAT IS "THE UMBRELLAS OF CHERBOURG"? | $400 |
| $600 | WHO IS (FEDERICO) FELLINI? | $600 |
| $800 | WHO IS AKIRA KUROSAWA? | $800 |
| $1000 | WHAT IS THE NETHERLANDS? (ACCEPT: HOLLAND) | $1000 |

# DOUBLE JEOPARDY!

## U.S. HISTORY

| Clue | Value | Response |
|------|-------|----------|
| FROM LATIN FOR "PUT AN END TO", THESE REFORMERS LIKE WILLIAM LLOYD GARRISON WANTED TO PUT AN END TO SLAVERY | $200 | WHAT ARE |
| THOROUGHLY RESTORED FOR ITS 100TH BIRTHDAY IN 1986, ITS TORCH WAS RELIT ON JULY 3 THAT YEAR | $400 | WHAT IS |
| ON JULY 2, 1932 FDR SAID, "I PLEDGE MYSELF TO" ONE OF THESE "FOR THE AMERICAN PEOPLE" | $600 | WHAT IS |
| IN 10 MINUTES, A MAY 31, 1889 FLOOD DESTROYED THIS PENNSYLVANIA TOWN & KILLED OVER 2,200 PEOPLE | $800 | WHAT IS |
| IN SEPTEMBER 1847 THIS GENERAL LED THE AMERICAN TROOPS THAT CAPTURED MEXICO CITY | $1000 | WHO IS |

# DOUBLE JEOPARDY!

## U.S. HISTORY

$200 — WHAT ARE ABOLITIONISTS? — $200

$400 — WHAT IS THE STATUE OF LIBERTY? — $400

$600 — WHAT IS "NEW DEAL"? — $600

$800 — WHAT IS JOHNSTOWN? — $800

$1000 — WHO IS WINFIELD SCOTT? — $1000

# DOUBLE JEOPARDY!

## MEET AL GORE

| | | |
|---|---|---|
| ENLISTING IN 1969, GORE SERVED AS AN ARMY REPORTER IN THIS FOREIGN COUNTRY | **$200** | WHAT IS |
| THIS FILM STAR SEEN IN "THE FUGITIVE" & "MEN IN BLACK" WAS AL'S ROOMMATE AT HARVARD | **$400** | WHO IS |
| AUTHOR ERICH SEGAL SAYS OLIVER BARRETT IV IN THIS 1970 NOVEL WAS PARTLY BASED ON AL | **$600** | WHAT IS |
| AL'S 1992 TREATISE ON THE ENVIRONMENT WAS TITLED THIS "IN THE BALANCE" | **$800** | WHAT IS |
| THE GORES' OLDEST DAUGHTER, SHE MARRIED A DOCTOR IN 1997 | **$1000** | WHO IS |

# DOUBLE JEOPARDY!

## MEET AL GORE

| | | |
|---|---|---|
| **$200** | WHAT IS (SOUTH) VIETNAM? | **$200** |
| **$400** | WHO IS TOMMY LEE JONES? | **$400** |
| **$600** | WHAT IS "LOVE STORY"? | **$600** |
| **$800** | WHAT IS EARTH? | **$800** |
| **$1000** | WHO IS KARENNA (GORE SCHIFF)? | **$1000** |

# DOUBLE JEOPARDY!

## GRAMMAR

| | | |
|---|---|---|
| THIS TYPE OF WORD OFTEN ENDS WITH -LY, BUT NOT IN PHRASES LIKE "OFTEN ENDS" | **$200** | WHAT IS |
| THE PROHIBITION ON SPLITTING THESE MAY DERIVE FROM THE FACT THAT IN LATIN THEY'RE ONE WORD | **$400** | WHAT ARE |
| A CLAUSE THAT MODIFIES A MAIN CLAUSE, OR A TERM FOR A SOLDIER OF LOWER RANK THAN ANOTHER | **$600** | WHAT IS |
| SOMETIMES IGNORED IN ENGLISH, IT'S THE MOOD OF HYPOTHETICAL STATEMENTS, AS IN "IF I WERE KING" | **$800** | WHAT IS |
| THIS WORD FOR SENTENCES LIKE "YOU'VE GROWN ANOTHER FOOT" COMES FROM LATIN FOR "TO GO AROUND" | **$1000** | WHAT IS |

# DOUBLE JEOPARDY!

## GRAMMAR

| | | |
|---|---|---|
| **$200** | WHAT IS AN ADVERB? | **$200** |
| **$400** | WHAT ARE INFINITIVES? | **$400** |
| **$600** | WHAT IS SUBORDINATE? | **$600** |
| **$800** | WHAT IS THE SUBJUNCTIVE? | **$800** |
| **$1000** | WHAT IS AMBIGUOUS? (ACCEPT: AMBIGUITY) | **$1000** |

# FINAL JEOPARDY!

## INVENTORS

HE WAS INDUCTED INTO
THE INVENTORS HALL OF
FAME IN 1997 FOR INVENT-
ING THE SUPERCOMPUTER

WHO IS

# FINAL JEOPARDY!™

## INVENTORS

WHO IS
SEYMOUR CRAY?

# JEOPARDY!™

## HOT DATES

| | | |
|---|---|---|
| THEN THE WORLD'S LONGEST SUSPENSION BRIDGE, IT OPENED OVER THE EAST RIVER MAY 24, 1883 | **$100** | WHAT IS |
| DELIVERED NOVEMBER 19, 1863, IT LASTED ONLY 2 MINUTES | **$200** | WHAT IS |
| THIS AL CAPP COMIC STRIP MADE ITS LAST APPEARANCE NOVEMBER 13, 1977 | **$300** | WHAT IS |
| REFERRING TO THE STOCK MARKET CRASH ON OCTOBER 30, 1929, VARIETY RAN THE HEADLINE "WALL ST." DOES THIS | **$400** | WHAT IS |
| HE WAS LAST REPORTED ALIVE JULY 30, 1975 OUTSIDE A BLOOMFIELD TOWNSHIP, MICH. RESTAURANT | **$500** | WHO IS |

# JEOPARDY!

## HOT DATES

| | | |
|---|---|---|
| **$100** | WHAT IS THE BROOKLYN BRIDGE? | **$100** |
| **$200** | WHAT IS THE GETTYSBURG ADDRESS? | **$200** |
| **$300** | WHAT IS "LI'L ABNER"? | **$300** |
| **$400** | WHAT IS "LAYS AN EGG"? | **$400** |
| **$500** | WHO IS JAMES R. HOFFA? | **$500** |

# JEOPARDY!

## POTATOES

| | | |
|---|---|---|
| THE POTATO ORIGINATED ON THIS CONTINENT, WHERE IT WAS CULTIVATED BY THE INCAS | **$100** | WHAT IS |
| THE ORIGINAL VERSION OF THIS TOY INCLUDED FACIAL PIECES TO ATTACH TO A REAL SPUD | **$200** | WHAT IS |
| THE FUNGUS PHYTOPHTHORA INFESTANS CAUSED THIS HISTORIC IRISH TRAGEDY | **$300** | WHAT IS |
| IN 1853 CHEF GEORGE CRUM INVENTED THIS SNACK AS A JOKE WHEN A CUSTOMER SAID HIS FRIES WERE TOO THICK | **$400** | WHAT ARE |
| 5-LETTER WORD APPLIED TO THE POTATO AS THE OUTGROWTH OF AN UNDERGROUND STEM | **$500** | WHAT IS |

# JEOPARDY!

## POTATOES

| | | |
|---|---|---|
| **$100** | WHAT IS SOUTH AMERICA? | **$100** |
| **$200** | WHAT IS MR. POTATO HEAD? | **$200** |
| **$300** | WHAT IS THE (GREAT) (IRISH) POTATO FAMINE? (ACCEPT: BLIGHT) | **$300** |
| **$400** | WHAT ARE POTATO CHIPS? | **$400** |
| **$500** | WHAT IS TUBER? | **$500** |

# JEOPARDY!™

## WOMEN IN SPORTS

| | | |
|---|---|---|
| 400-METER STAR CATHY FREEMAN WAS THE FIRST OF THESE INDIGENOUS AUSTRALIANS TO WIN A WORLD TRACK GOLD MEDAL | **$100** | WHAT ARE |
| SHE HAD WON 7 OF 9 GRAND SLAM SINGLES EVENTS WHEN SHE WAS STABBED & WOUNDED IN 1993 | **$200** | WHO IS |
| PAULA NEWBY- FRASER COULD BE CALLED IRONWOMAN FOR WINNING THIS IRON-MAN EVENT 7 TIMES FROM 1986 TO 1994 | **$300** | WHAT IS |
| IN 1997 THIS GYMNAST WHO VAULTED HURT AT THE '96 OLYMPICS WENT TO ISRAEL FOR THE MACCABIAH GAMES | **$400** | WHO IS |
| IN 1993 MARGE SCHOTT, OWNER OF THIS TEAM, WAS SUSPENDED FOR MAK-ING RACIST REMARKS | **$500** | WHAT ARE |

# JEOPARDY!

## WOMEN IN SPORTS

$100 — WHAT ARE ABORIGINES? — $100

$200 — WHO IS MONICA SELES? — $200

$300 — WHAT IS THE (IRONMAN) TRIATHLON? — $300

$400 — WHO IS KERRI STRUG? — $400

$500 — WHAT ARE THE CINCINNATI REDS? — $500

# JEOPARDY!

## PEOPLE & PLACES

| | | |
|---|---|---|
| BAGHDADIS ARE CITIZENS OF THIS COUNTRY; WE DON'T KNOW WHERE THE BAGHMOMMIS LIVE | **$100** | WHAT IS |
| IT ISN'T INSULTING TO BE CALLED A GOPHER IF YOU LIVE IN THIS "GOPHER STATE" | **$200** | WHAT IS |
| THESE NOMADS CALL THEMSELVES THE ROM, WHICH MEANS "MAN" OR "HUSBAND" IN THEIR LANGUAGE, ROMANY | **$300** | WHO ARE |
| THE PEOPLE OF THIS "CONSTITUTION STATE" ARE CALLED NUTMEGS OR NUTMEGGERS | **$400** | WHAT IS |
| CANADIANS ARE FROM CANADA; CANARIANS ARE FROM THE CANARY ISLANDS, PART OF THIS COUNTRY | **$500** | WHAT IS |

# JEOPARDY!

## PEOPLE & PLACES

$100     WHAT IS IRAQ?     $100

$200     WHAT IS MINNESOTA?     $200

$300     WHO ARE THE GYPSIES?     $300

$400     WHAT IS CONNECTICUT?     $400

$500     WHAT IS SPAIN?     $500

# JEOPARDY!

## LITERARY HODGEPODGE

| | | |
|---|---|---|
| THIS 1939 STEINBECK NOVEL ABOUT A FAMILY OF MIGRANT WORKERS WON THE PULITZER PRIZE FOR FICTION | **$100** | WHAT IS |
| WORDSWORTH'S POEM ABOUT HER BEGINS, "HAIL, VIRGIN QUEEN! O'ER MANY AN ENVIOUS BAR TRIUMPHANT..." | **$200** | WHO IS |
| TITLE CHARACTER WHO SAYS, "I SHALL GROW OLD...AND DREADFUL. BUT THIS PICTURE WILL REMAIN ALWAYS YOUNG" | **$300** | WHO IS |
| THE MINISTRY OF LOVE, ALSO KNOWN AS MINILUV, MAINTAINS LAW & ORDER IN THIS ORWELL NOVEL | **$400** | WHAT IS |
| JOHN UPDIKE CHARACTER WHOSE NAME PRECEDES "RUN", "REDUX", "IS RICH" & "AT REST" | **$500** | WHO IS |

# JEOPARDY!

## LITERARY HODGEPODGE

| | | |
|---|---|---|
| **$100** | WHAT IS "THE GRAPES OF WRATH"? | **$100** |
| **$200** | WHO IS ELIZABETH I? | **$200** |
| **$300** | WHO IS DORIAN GRAY? | **$300** |
| **$400** | WHAT IS "1984"? | **$400** |
| **$500** | WHO IS RABBIT (ANGSTROM)? | **$500** |

# JEOPARDY!

## 10-LETTER WORDS

| Clue | Value | Response |
|------|-------|----------|
| IT'S A STATEMENT OF WHAT A THING IS, & CAN ALSO REFER TO CLEARLY OUTLINED MUSCLES | $100 | WHAT IS |
| IN A CRIMINAL TRIAL, IT'S THIS LAWYER'S JOB TO TRY & PROVE THE DEFENDANT GUILTY | $200 | WHO IS |
| IT'S EQUAL TO .0394 INCHES | $300 | WHAT IS |
| IT'S THE PIGMENT THAT MAKES RED BLOOD CELLS RED | $400 | WHAT IS |
| A CREATURE THAT EATS BOTH ANIMALS & PLANTS IS DESCRIBED BY THIS ADJECTIVE | $500 | WHAT IS |

37

# JEOPARDY!

# 10-LETTER WORDS

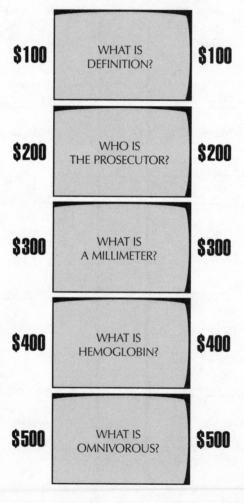

| | | |
|---|---|---|
| **$100** | WHAT IS DEFINITION? | **$100** |
| **$200** | WHO IS THE PROSECUTOR? | **$200** |
| **$300** | WHAT IS A MILLIMETER? | **$300** |
| **$400** | WHAT IS HEMOGLOBIN? | **$400** |
| **$500** | WHAT IS OMNIVOROUS? | **$500** |

# DOUBLE JEOPARDY!

## BALLET

| | | |
|---|---|---|
| THIS HEROINE'S STEPSISTERS TRY TO SQUEEZE THEIR BIG FEET INTO HER GLASS SLIPPER, BUT THEY DON'T FIT | **$200** | WHO IS |
| THIS LATE BALLET STAR OF TARTAR ANCESTRY WAS MARGOT FONTEYN'S BEST-KNOWN PARTNER | **$400** | WHO IS |
| THIS TROUPE WAS FIRST ORGANIZED IN MOSCOW IN THE 1770s | **$600** | WHAT IS |
| 1-WORD TITLE OF AARON COPLAND'S 1942 BALLET INSPIRED BY AMERICAN FOLK TUNES | **$800** | WHAT IS |
| THE EROTIC ENDING OF THIS GREAT DANCER'S 1912 BALLET "L'APRES-MIDI D'UN FAUNE" CREATED A SCANDAL | **$1000** | WHO IS |

# DOUBLE JEOPARDY!

## BALLET

**$200**  WHO IS CINDERELLA? (ACCEPT: CENDRILLON)  **$200**

**$400**  WHO IS RUDOLF NUREYEV?  **$400**

**$600**  WHAT IS THE BOLSHOI (BALLET OR THEATER)?  **$600**

**$800**  WHAT IS "RODEO"?  **$800**

**$1000**  WHO IS VASLAV NIJINSKY?  **$1000**

# DOUBLE JEOPARDY!

## THAT'S COOL

| | | |
|---|---|---|
| ONE REVIEW OF THIS 1967 FILM SAID NEWMAN PLAYS "A TOUGH NUT" WHO "REFUSES TO CRACK UNDER PRESSURE" | **$200** | WHAT IS |
| KRAFT WARNS NOT TO USE THE MICROWAVE TO THAW THIS DESSERT TOPPER, FIRST SOLD NATIONALLY IN 1968 | **$400** | WHAT IS |
| WHILE YOU TWIDDLE YOUR THUMBS, IT'S THESE BODY PARTS YOU "COOL" | **$600** | WHAT ARE |
| BORN ARTIS IVEY JR., THIS FATHER OF 6 PICKED UP THE 1995 BEST RAP SOLO PERFORMANCE GRAMMY | **$800** | WHO IS |
| IT WAS THE REPUBLICANS' 4-WORD SLOGAN IN THE 1924 PRESIDENTIAL CAMPAIGN | **$1000** | WHAT IS |

# DOUBLE JEOPARDY!

## THAT'S COOL

$200 — WHAT IS "COOL HAND LUKE"? — $200

$400 — WHAT IS COOL WHIP? — $400

$600 — WHAT ARE YOUR HEELS? — $600

$800 — WHO IS COOLIO? — $800

$1000 — WHAT IS "KEEP COOL WITH COOLIDGE"? — $1000

# DOUBLE JEOPARDY!

## JOHN CUSACK MOVIES

| | | |
|---|---|---|
| NICOLAS CAGE & JOHN CUSACK TEAM UP WHEN INMATES HIJACK A PLANE IN THIS 1997 THRILLER | **$200** | WHAT IS |
| CUSACK WAS THE VOICE OF DIMITRI IN THIS 1997 ANIMATED FILM ABOUT A RUSSIAN PRINCESS | **$400** | WHAT IS |
| IN AN OFFBEAT 1999 FILM, PUPPETEER CUSACK DISCOVERS A PORTAL INTO THIS FAMOUS ACTOR'S BRAIN | **$600** | WHO IS |
| CUSACK WAS THIRD BASEMAN BUCK WEAVER IN THIS 1988 FILM ABOUT THE BLACK SOX SCANDAL | **$800** | WHAT IS |
| CUSACK STARRED WITH MINNIE DRIVER IN THIS 1997 MOVIE ABOUT A MICHIGAN HIGH SCHOOL REUNION | **$1000** | WHAT IS |

# DOUBLE JEOPARDY!

## JOHN CUSACK MOVIES

| | | |
|---|---|---|
| $200 | WHAT IS "CON AIR"? | $200 |
| $400 | WHAT IS "ANASTASIA"? | $400 |
| $600 | WHO IS JOHN MALKOVICH? | $600 |
| $800 | WHAT IS "EIGHT MEN OUT"? | $800 |
| $1000 | WHAT IS "GROSSE POINTE BLANK"? | $1000 |

# DOUBLE JEOPARDY!

## CRUSTACEANS

| | | |
|---|---|---|
| BIG ONES (WHICH IS KIND OF AN OXYMORON) ARE CALLED PRAWNS | **$200** | WHAT ARE |
| WATCH OUT FOR THE GOOSE TYPE OF THESE; THEY MAY GROW ATTACHED TO THE HULL OF YOUR SHIP | **$400** | WHAT ARE |
| THE DUNGENESS TYPE OF THIS CRUSTACEAN HAS THE SCIENTIFIC NAME CANCER MAGISTER | **$600** | WHAT IS |
| CRUSTACEAN THAT'S THE TITLE OF A 1979 B-52'S SONG | **$800** | WHAT IS |
| BLUE WHALES EAT TONS OF THESE TINY CRUSTACEANS WHOSE NAME IS FROM THE NORWEGIAN FOR A FISH'S YOUNG | **$1000** | WHAT ARE |

# DOUBLE JEOPARDY!

## CRUSTACEANS

| | |
|---|---|
| **$200** | WHAT ARE SHRIMP? |
| **$400** | WHAT ARE BARNACLES? (ACCEPT: CIRRIPEDS) |
| **$600** | WHAT IS A CRAB? |
| **$800** | WHAT IS A ROCK LOBSTER? |
| **$1000** | WHAT ARE KRILL? |

# DOUBLE JEOPARDY!

## ST. LOUIS

| | | |
|---|---|---|
| FAMILIAR SHAPE OF THE JEFFERSON NATIONAL EXPANSION MEMORIAL'S "GATEWAY" | **$200** | WHAT IS |
| THIS RAGTIME COMPOSER'S HOME AT 2658A DELMAR BLVD. HAS BEEN RESTORED & OPENED FOR TOURS | **$400** | WHO IS |
| FOR ALMOST 30 YEARS THIS CHEVY SPORTS CAR, INCLUDING THE STING RAY, WAS BUILT IN ST. LOUIS | **$600** | WHAT IS |
| THIS COMPANY'S FAMOUS CHECKER- BOARD SQUARE IS IN ST. LOUIS | **$800** | WHAT IS |
| THIS ST. LOUIS UNIVERSITY FOUNDED IN 1853 HAS A 169-ACRE HILLTOP CAMPUS | **$1000** | WHAT IS |

# DOUBLE JEOPARDY!

## ST. LOUIS

| | | |
|---|---|---|
| $200 | WHAT IS AN ARCH? | $200 |
| $400 | WHO IS SCOTT JOPLIN? | $400 |
| $600 | WHAT IS THE CORVETTE? | $600 |
| $800 | WHAT IS RALSTON PURINA? (ACCEPT: PURINA) | $800 |
| $1000 | WHAT IS WASHINGTON UNIVERSITY? | $1000 |

# DOUBLE JEOPARDY!

## BEFORE & AFTER

| | | |
|---|---|---|
| 1961 INVASION OF CUBA WRAPPED IN A TASTY PASTRY | **$200** | WHAT IS |
| THE LEAD SINGER OF HOLE APPEARING ON CHUCK WOOLERY'S OLD DATING SHOW | **$400** | WHO IS |
| LONG DISPUTED ISRAELI-PALESTINIAN LAND AREA THAT'S A MINI-SHOPPING COMPLEX | **$600** | WHAT IS |
| KING KONG PLUNGES FROM EDWARD GIBBON'S MASSIVE HISTORY | **$800** | WHAT IS |
| JIMMY CARTER'S "ACHY BREAKY" SECRETARY OF STATE | **$1000** | WHO IS |

# DOUBLE JEOPARDY!™

## BEFORE & AFTER

$200 — WHAT IS BAY OF PIGS IN A BLANKET? — $200

$400 — WHO IS COURTNEY LOVE CONNECTION? — $400

$600 — WHAT IS THE GAZA STRIP MALL? — $600

$800 — WHAT IS THE DECLINE & FALL OF THE ROMAN EMPIRE STATE BUILDING? — $800

$1000 — WHO IS BILLY RAY CYRUS VANCE? — $1000

# FINAL JEOPARDY!

## FAMOUS AMERICAN FAMILIES

IN HARTFORD OVER 200
MANHOLE COVERS MADE
FROM CONFISCATED GUNS
ARE ENGRAVED WITH THE
MOTTO OF THIS LOCAL
FAMILY

WHO ARE

# FINAL JEOPARDY!

## FAMOUS AMERICAN FAMILIES

WHO ARE THE COLTS?

# JEOPARDY!

## THE WHITE HOUSE

| | | |
|---|---|---|
| IT'S THE WHITE HOUSE'S STREET ADDRESS | **$100** | WHAT IS |
| IT'S THE SHAPE OF THE BLUE ROOM AS WELL AS OF A FAMOUS OFFICE | **$200** | WHAT IS |
| THE EMANCIPATION PROCLAMATION WAS SIGNED IN THIS FAMOUS ROOM; MAYBE YOU'VE SLEPT THERE | **$300** | WHAT IS |
| THE WHITE HOUSE WASN'T YET FINISHED IN 1800 WHEN THIS PRESIDENT MOVED IN | **$400** | WHO IS |
| THIS PRESIDENT HUNG A LARGE MOOSE HEAD IN THE STATE DINING ROOM; A BULL MOOSE, WE PRESUME | **$500** | WHO IS |

# JEOPARDY!

## THE WHITE HOUSE

| | |
|---|---|
| **$100** | WHAT IS 1600 PENNSYLVANIA AVENUE? | **$100** |
| **$200** | WHAT IS OVAL? | **$200** |
| **$300** | WHAT IS THE LINCOLN BEDROOM? (ACCEPT: LINCOLN ROOM) | **$300** |
| **$400** | WHO IS JOHN ADAMS? | **$400** |
| **$500** | WHO IS THEODORE ROOSEVELT? | **$500** |

# JEOPARDY!

## UNMENTIONABLES

| | | |
|---|---|---|
| ANTONIO SABATO JR. WORE THIS DESIGNER'S BLACK BIKINI BRIEFS ON A 90-FOOT BILLBOARD IN TIMES SQUARE | **$100** | WHO IS |
| ITS TRADEMARK IS COMPOSED OF AN APPLE, GRAPES, GOOSEBERRIES & A CLUSTER OF LEAVES | **$200** | WHAT IS |
| TYRA BANKS & CLAUDIA SCHIFFER HAVE GRACED THE COVER OF THIS COLUMBUS, OHIO-BASED LINGERIE CATALOG | **$300** | WHAT IS |
| MADONNA'S BUSTIER WAS STOLEN FROM THIS HOLLYWOOD STORE'S LINGERIE MUSEUM DURING THE 1992 L.A. RIOTS | **$400** | WHAT IS |
| BVD MADE THIS ONE-PIECE, LONG-SLEEVED UNDERGARMENT; YOU NEEDN'T BE A TEAMSTER TO WEAR IT | **$500** | WHAT IS |

# JEOPARDY!

## UNMENTIONABLES

| | | |
|---|---|---|
| **$100** | WHO IS CALVIN KLEIN? | **$100** |
| **$200** | WHAT IS FRUIT OF THE LOOM? | **$200** |
| **$300** | WHAT IS VICTORIA'S SECRET? | **$300** |
| **$400** | WHAT IS FREDERICK'S OF HOLLYWOOD? | **$400** |
| **$500** | WHAT IS A UNION SUIT? | **$500** |

# JEOPARDY!

## VERSE

| Clue | Value | Response |
|------|-------|----------|
| 3-LETTER WORD THAT ENDS ERNEST THAYER'S POEM "CASEY AT THE BAT" | $100 | WHAT IS |
| HE WROTE, "I HEAR AMERICA SINGING, THE VARIED CAROLS I HEAR" | $200 | WHO IS |
| IN "EVERYTHING IN ITS PLACE", ARTHUR GUITERMAN WROTE, "THE BIRDS ARE IN THE BUSHES AND" THIS "IS AT THE DOOR" | $300 | WHAT IS |
| HE'S THE REGIMENTAL BHISTI, OR WATER CARRIER, THAT RUDYARD KIPLING MADE FAMOUS | $400 | WHO IS |
| IN A ROBERT FROST POEM, A NEIGHBOR INSISTS THESE "MAKE GOOD NEIGHBORS" | $500 | WHAT ARE |

# JEOPARDY!

## VERSE

$100 — WHAT IS OUT? — $100

$200 — WHO IS WALT WHITMAN? — $200

$300 — WHAT IS THE WOLF? — $300

$400 — WHO IS GUNGA DIN? — $400

$500 — WHAT ARE GOOD FENCES? — $500

# JEOPARDY!

## FAMOUS LATINOS

| Clue | Value | Response |
|---|---|---|
| HIS "VIDA LOCA" HAS INCLUDED TOURS OF DUTY WITH MENUDO & ON "GENERAL HOSPITAL" | **$100** | WHO IS |
| THE GOLDEN BOY OF THE 1992 OLYMPICS WAS THIS LIGHTWEIGHT BOXER | **$200** | WHO IS |
| THIS ONETIME "NYPD BLUE" STAR WAS BORN IN BROOKLYN IN 1955 | **$300** | WHO IS |
| HE LED A JULY 26, 1953 ATTACK ON THE MONCADA ARMY BARRACKS IN SANTIAGO DE CUBA | **$400** | WHO IS |
| REVLON ADDED THIS VOLUPTUOUS "FOOLS RUSH IN" STAR TO ITS STABLE OF MODELS | **$500** | WHO IS |

# JEOPARDY!

## FAMOUS LATINOS

| $100 | WHO IS RICKY MARTIN? | $100 |

| $200 | WHO IS OSCAR DE LA HOYA? | $200 |

| $300 | WHO IS JIMMY SMITS? | $300 |

| $400 | WHO IS FIDEL CASTRO? | $400 |

| $500 | WHO IS SALMA HAYEK? | $500 |

# JEOPARDY!

## MUSTY TV

| | | |
|---|---|---|
| ELIZABETH MONTGOMERY PLAYED QUIRKY COUSIN SERENA AS WELL AS SAMANTHA ON THIS SITCOM | **$100** | WHAT IS |
| AS PLAYED BY AL LEWIS, GRANDPA ON THIS FAMILY SITCOM COULD TURN INTO A BAT | **$200** | WHAT IS |
| AN ASSASSIN'S BULLET PARALYZED THIS DETECTIVE PLAYED BY RAYMOND BURR | **$300** | WHO IS |
| ON TV THIS GERMAN SHEPHERD SERVED AS A PRIVATE IN THE U.S. CAVALRY | **$400** | WHO IS |
| ABE VIGODA PLAYED THIS DETECTIVE ON "BARNEY MILLER" & A SPIN-OFF | **$500** | WHO IS |

# JEOPARDY!

## MUSTY TV

**$100**   WHAT IS "BEWITCHED"?   **$100**

**$200**   WHAT IS "THE MUNSTERS"?   **$200**

**$300**   WHO IS (ROBERT) IRONSIDE?   **$300**

**$400**   WHO IS RIN TIN TIN? (ACCEPT: RINTIE)   **$400**

**$500**   WHO IS (PHIL) FISH?   **$500**

# JEOPARDY!

## HOMOPHONES

| | | |
|---|---|---|
| ANOTHER NAME FOR A BUCKET, OR YOUR COLORING IF ONE FALLS ON YOU | **$100** | WHAT IS |
| YOU OPEN IT IN A FIREPLACE, OR IT MAY MEAN YOU'RE ALREADY WAY TOO WARM | **$200** | WHAT IS |
| A CAUSTIC SUBSTANCE IN SOAP, OR AN UNTRUTH | **$300** | WHAT IS |
| A TYPE OF SANDWICH BREAD, OR TWISTED, LIKE A SENSE OF HUMOR | **$400** | WHAT IS |
| IT'S A CORRIDOR, OR HOW YOU MIGHT CARRY SOMETHING DOWN ONE | **$500** | WHAT IS |

# JEOPARDY!

## HOMOPHONES

| | | |
|---|---|---|
| $100 | WHAT IS PAIL/PALE? | $100 |
| $200 | WHAT IS FLUE/FLU? | $200 |
| $300 | WHAT IS LYE/LIE? | $300 |
| $400 | WHAT IS WRY/RYE? | $400 |
| $500 | WHAT IS HALL/HAUL? | $500 |

# DOUBLE JEOPARDY!

## THE COSSACKS ARE COMING!

| Clue | Value | Response |
|------|-------|----------|
| FOR HIS BOOKS ON THE COSSACKS OF THE DON RIVER, MIKHAIL SHOLOKHOV WON THIS TOP PRIZE IN 1965 | **$200** | WHAT IS |
| WHILE THERE WERE A FEW MECHANIZED UNITS, THE COSSACKS IN WWII MAINLY SERVED IN THESE UNITS | **$400** | WHAT ARE |
| FOR A WHILE THE CITY OF KHARKIV, FOUNDED AS A COSSACK OUT-POST, REPLACED KIEV AS CAPITAL OF THIS REPUBLIC | **$600** | WHAT IS |
| IN 1992 THIS RUSSIAN PRESIDENT GRANTED THE COSSACKS THE STATUS OF AN ETHNIC GROUP | **$800** | WHO IS |
| THE NAME COSSACK COMES FROM "KAZAK", A WORD IN THIS LANGUAGE THAT ALSO GAVE US THE WORD YOGURT | **$1000** | WHAT IS |

# DOUBLE JEOPARDY!

## THE COSSACKS ARE COMING!

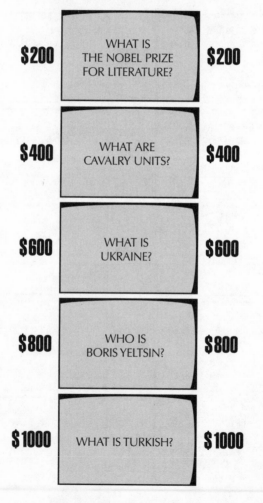

**$200**  WHAT IS THE NOBEL PRIZE FOR LITERATURE?  **$200**

**$400**  WHAT ARE CAVALRY UNITS?  **$400**

**$600**  WHAT IS UKRAINE?  **$600**

**$800**  WHO IS BORIS YELTSIN?  **$800**

**$1000**  WHAT IS TURKISH?  **$1000**

# DOUBLE JEOPARDY!

## PSYCH 102

| Clue | Value | Response |
|---|---|---|
| THE "WRITER'S" TYPE IS A COMMON FORM OF THIS, A PSYCHO-LOGICAL OBSTACLE TO COMPLETING A PROJECT | **$200** | WHAT IS |
| BIPOLAR DISORDER IS AN ILLNESS COMMONLY REFERRED TO AS "MANIC" THIS | **$400** | WHAT IS |
| THIS COGNITIVE PROCESS HAS 3 STAGES: ACQUISITION, RETENTION & RETRIEVAL | **$600** | WHAT IS |
| IN WWI, "POST- TRAU-MATIC STRESS DISOR-DER" WAS KNOWN AS "COMBAT FATIGUE" OR THIS ALLITERATIVE 2-WORD TERM | **$800** | WHAT IS |
| 2-LETTER FREUDIAN TERM FOR THE DEEP PART OF THE PSYCHE GOVERNED BY THE PLEASURE PRINCIPLE | **$1000** | WHAT IS |

# DOUBLE JEOPARDY!

## PSYCH 102

| | | |
|---|---|---|
| $200 | WHAT IS A BLOCK? | $200 |
| $400 | WHAT IS DEPRESSION? | $400 |
| $600 | WHAT IS MEMORY? | $600 |
| $800 | WHAT IS SHELL SHOCK? | $800 |
| $1000 | WHAT IS THE ID? | $1000 |

# DOUBLE JEOPARDY!

## 1960s MUSIC

| Clue | Value | Response |
|------|-------|----------|
| IN 1968 THIS DUO SERENADED MRS. ROBINSON | **$200** | WHO ARE |
| IN 1963 JIMMY GILMER HIT NO. 1 WITH "SUGAR SHACK"; IN 1969 THIS GROUP HIT NO. 1 WITH "SUGAR SUGAR" | **$400** | WHAT ARE |
| DUE TO AN OWNERSHIP DISPUTE, THIS 1966 NO. 1 HIT BY THE TROGGS WAS RELEASED SIMULTANEOUSLY ON 2 LABELS | **$600** | WHAT IS |
| THIS GROUP'S 1965 HIT "DO YOU BELIEVE IN MAGIC" WAS USED IN 1990s TV COMMERCIALS BY McDONALD'S | **$800** | WHO IS |
| THIS 1963 HIT BY KYU SAKAMOTO WAS RELEASED IN JAPAN AS "UE O MUITE ARUKO", OR "I LOOK UP WHEN I WALK" | **$1000** | WHAT IS |

# DOUBLE JEOPARDY!

## 1960s MUSIC

| | | |
|---|---|---|
| **$200** | WHO ARE SIMON & GARFUNKEL? | **$200** |
| **$400** | WHAT ARE THE ARCHIES? | **$400** |
| **$600** | WHAT IS "WILD THING"? | **$600** |
| **$800** | WHAT IS THE LOVIN' SPOONFUL? | **$800** |
| **$1000** | WHAT IS "SUKIYAKI"? | **$1000** |

# DOUBLE JEOPARDY!

## SCOOPS

| | | |
|---|---|---|
| IN 1936 EDGAR SNOW REACHED SHAANXI PROVINCE & GOT AN INTERVIEW WITH THIS FUTURE CHAIRMAN | **$200** | WHO IS |
| IN 1945 REPORTER WILLIAM LAURENCE GOT TO FLY OVER THIS CITY FOR THE SECOND A-BOMB DROP | **$400** | WHAT IS |
| REPORTER ANDREA MITCHELL GOT THE SCOOP THAT GEORGE BUSH HAD MADE THIS CONTROVERSIAL CHOICE AUG. 16, 1988 | **$600** | WHAT IS |
| THE REGISTER OF THIS COUNTY NEAR L.A. WON A 1996 PULITZER FOR REPORTING ON FERTILITY CLINIC FRAUD | **$800** | WHAT IS |
| AMONG SCOOPS BY THIS "WASHINGTON MERRY-GO-ROUND" COLUMNIST WERE FACTS LEADING TO THE CENSURE OF SEN. THOMAS DODD | **$1000** | WHO IS |

# DOUBLE JEOPARDY!

## SCOOPS

$200 — WHO IS MAO TSE-TUNG? — $200

$400 — WHAT IS NAGASAKI? — $400

$600 — WHAT IS DAN QUAYLE (FOR RUNNING MATE)? — $600

$800 — WHAT IS ORANGE COUNTY? — $800

$1000 — WHO IS JACK ANDERSON? (ACCEPT: DREW PEARSON) — $1000

# DOUBLE JEOPARDY!

## FARAWAY PLACES

| | | |
|---|---|---|
| TIMBUKTU IN MALI WAS ONCE A MAJOR CARAVAN CENTER FOR THOSE CROSSING THIS DESERT | **$200** | WHAT IS |
| THIS REMOTE ASIAN NATION ONCE HAD "OUTER" ATTACHED TO ITS NAME; AN "INNER" REGION BELONGS TO CHINA | **$400** | WHAT IS |
| TOURS IN THIS FAR-AWAY LAND INCLUDE A SAFARI IN ROYAL CHITWAN NATIONAL PARK & RAFTING TRIPS NEAR KATMANDU | **$600** | WHAT IS |
| PUNTA ARENAS, IN THIS COUNTRY, IS THE WORLD'S SOUTHERN-MOST CITY ON A CONTINENTAL MAINLAND | **$800** | WHAT IS |
| A CITY "UZ"ING CULTURE, SAMARKAND IN THIS FORMER SOVIET REPUBLIC IS THE SITE OF TAMERLANE'S TOMB | **$1000** | WHAT IS |

# DOUBLE JEOPARDY!

## FARAWAY PLACES

| | | |
|---|---|---|
| $200 | WHAT IS THE SAHARA? | $200 |
| $400 | WHAT IS MONGOLIA? | $400 |
| $600 | WHAT IS NEPAL? | $600 |
| $800 | WHAT IS CHILE? | $800 |
| $1000 | WHAT IS UZBEKISTAN? | $1000 |

# DOUBLE JEOPARDY!

## GOING "STRAIGHT"

| | | |
|---|---|---|
| A POKER HAND CONSISTING OF THE 6, 5, 4, 3 & 2 OF CLUBS | $200 | WHAT IS |
| A PIECE OF WOOD OR METAL, LIKE A RULER, THAT CAN BE USED TO DRAW UNWAVERING LINES | $400 | WHAT IS |
| GRACIE ALLEN WAS MARRIED TO HERS | $600 | WHAT IS |
| 1999 DAVID LYNCH FILM ABOUT AN ELDERLY MAN'S TRIP TO VISIT HIS BROTHER | $800 | WHAT IS |
| IN POLITICAL LINGO, TO "VOTE" THIS IS TO SUBMIT A BALLOT SUPPORTING CANDIDATES OF JUST ONE PARTY | $1000 | WHAT IS |

75

# DOUBLE JEOPARDY!

## GOING "STRAIGHT"

| | | |
|:---:|:---:|:---:|
| **$200** | WHAT IS A STRAIGHT FLUSH? | **$200** |
| **$400** | WHAT IS A STRAIGHTEDGE? | **$400** |
| **$600** | WHAT IS A STRAIGHT MAN? | **$600** |
| **$800** | WHAT IS "THE STRAIGHT STORY"? | **$800** |
| **$1000** | WHAT IS THE STRAIGHT TICKET? | **$1000** |

# FINAL JEOPARDY!

## STATE CAPITALS

IN 1765 THIS CITY WAS
NAMED IN HONOR OF THE
PEACEFUL RESOLUTION OF
A BOUNDARY DISPUTE

WHAT IS

# FINAL JEOPARDY!
## STATE CAPITALS

WHAT IS CONCORD
(NEW HAMPSHIRE)?

# JEOPARDY!

## MARCH OF TIME

| | | |
|---|---|---|
| ONCE HOME TO AL CAPONE & A BIRDMAN, IT CLOSED ITS CELL DOORS MARCH 21, 1963 | **$100** | WHAT IS |
| ON MARCH 25, 1957 6 COUNTRIES SIGNED THE TREATY OF ROME TO FORM THIS, THE EEC | **$200** | WHAT IS |
| ON MARCH 8, 1999 SCIENTIST WEN HO LEE WAS FIRED FROM THIS NEW MEXICO NATIONAL LABORATORY | **$300** | WHAT IS |
| THE U.S. VOTED AGAINST JOINING THIS ORGANIZATION MARCH 19, 1920; TODAY WE'RE HERE & IT ISN'T | **$400** | WHAT IS |
| ON MARCH 1, 1954 THE U.S. CONDUCTED THE FIRST OF A SERIES OF HYDROGEN BOMB TESTS ON THIS PACIFIC ATOLL | **$500** | WHAT IS |

# JEOPARDY!

## MARCH OF TIME

**$100**  WHAT IS ALCATRAZ?  **$100**

**$200**  WHAT IS THE EUROPEAN ECONOMIC COMMUNITY?  **$200**

**$300**  WHAT IS LOS ALAMOS?  **$300**

**$400**  WHAT IS THE LEAGUE OF NATIONS?  **$400**

**$500**  WHAT IS BIKINI ATOLL?  **$500**

# JEOPARDY!™

## BLACK AMERICANS

| | | |
|---|---|---|
| IN 1989, AT AGE 52, HE BECAME THE YOUNGEST MAN EVER TO SERVE AS CHAIRMAN OF THE JOINT CHIEFS OF STAFF | **$100** | WHO IS |
| THIS MONTGOMERY SEAMSTRESS WAS THROWN OFF A BUS ONE OTHER TIME BEFORE HER FAMOUS DEC. 1, 1955 INCIDENT | **$200** | WHO IS |
| THIS KILLER COMIC HAS SHOWN HE CAN "BRING THE PAIN" & BE PART OF THE "LETHAL WEAPON" FRANCHISE | **$300** | WHO IS |
| THIS AUTHOR OF "I KNOW WHY THE CAGED BIRD SINGS" WON THE NAACP'S SPINGARN MEDAL IN 1994 | **$400** | WHO IS |
| ONCE WHITE HOUSE DIRECTOR OF PUBLIC LIAISON, SHE BECAME THE USA'S FIRST BLACK SECRETARY OF LABOR IN 1997 | **$500** | WHO IS |

# JEOPARDY!

## BLACK AMERICANS

| | | |
|---|---|---|
| $100 | WHO IS COLIN POWELL? | $100 |
| $200 | WHO IS ROSA PARKS? | $200 |
| $300 | WHO IS CHRIS ROCK? | $300 |
| $400 | WHO IS MAYA ANGELOU? | $400 |
| $500 | WHO IS ALEXIS HERMAN? | $500 |

# JEOPARDY!™

## ASSOCIATES

| Clue | Value | Response |
|---|---|---|
| AN ASSOCIATE OF EQUAL RANK; YOU MAY BE A "JOLLY GOOD" ONE | $100 | WHAT IS |
| IT CAN REFER TO AN INTIMATE FRIEND OR TO A COMMUNIST | $200 | WHAT IS |
| THE FAMILIAL NAME FOR A CO-MEMBER OF A MEN'S GREEK LETTER ASSOCIATION | $300 | WHAT IS |
| FROM A WORD FOR "TO LABOR TOGETHER", IT'S ONE WHO HELPS THE ENEMY FORCE OCCUPYING HIS COUNTRY | $400 | WHAT IS |
| PERHAPS FROM THE GREEK FOR "TIME", IT'S A LONGTIME "OLD" PAL | $500 | WHAT IS |

# JEOPARDY!

## ASSOCIATES

| | | |
|---|---|---|
| **$100** | WHAT IS A FELLOW? | **$100** |
| **$200** | WHAT IS COMRADE? | **$200** |
| **$300** | WHAT IS A FRAT(ERNITY) BROTHER? | **$300** |
| **$400** | WHAT IS A COLLABORATOR? | **$400** |
| **$500** | WHAT IS A CRONY? | **$500** |

# JEOPARDY!

## HISTORIC NAMES

| Clue | Value | Response |
|---|---|---|
| ONE OF THE SIGNERS OF ISRAEL'S DECLARATION OF INDEPENDENCE, SHE BECAME PRIME MINISTER IN 1969 | **$100** | WHO IS |
| BEFORE DESIGNING THE FIRST SUCCESSFUL STEAMBOAT, HE WORKED AS A PORTRAIT PAINTER | **$200** | WHO IS |
| THIS "NINE DAYS' QUEEN" OF ENGLAND WAS A GRAND-DAUGHTER OF HENRY VIII's SISTER MARY | **$300** | WHO IS |
| THIS REDSHIRTS LEADER LED HIS FINAL CAMPAIGN WHEN HE FOUGHT FOR FRANCE IN THE FRANCO-PRUSSIAN WAR | **$400** | WHO IS |
| A SIOUX LEADER AT THE TIME OF THE LITTLE BIGHORN, HIS INDIAN NAME WAS TATANKA YOTANKA | **$500** | WHO IS |

# JEOPARDY!™

## HISTORIC NAMES

| | | |
|---|---|---|
| **$100** | WHO IS GOLDA MEIR? | **$100** |
| **$200** | WHO IS ROBERT FULTON? | **$200** |
| **$300** | WHO IS (LADY) JANE GREY? | **$300** |
| **$400** | WHO IS GIUSEPPE GARIBALDI? | **$400** |
| **$500** | WHO IS SITTING BULL? | **$500** |

# JEOPARDY!

## EUROPEAN VACATION

| | | |
|---|---|---|
| ACCORDING TO THE MOVIES, THIS LANDMARK IS VISIBLE FROM EVERY WINDOW IN EVERY BUILDING IN PARIS | **$100** | WHAT IS |
| IN THIS CZECH CAPITAL, YOU CAN VISIT A HOME WHERE MOZART COMPOSED PART OF "DON GIOVANNI" | **$200** | WHAT IS |
| WHILE IN ROME, IT'S POSSIBLE TO STAND WITH ONE FOOT IN EACH OF THESE COUNTRIES | **$300** | WHAT ARE |
| TO SEE HIS "NIGHT WATCH", HEAD TO THE RIJKSMUSEUM IN AMSTERDAM | **$400** | WHO IS |
| WHILE MOM'S AT CHRISTIANSBORG PALACE IN THIS CITY, DAD MAY HEAD DOWN THE STREET TO THE EROTIC MUSEUM | **$500** | WHAT IS |

# JEOPARDY!

## EUROPEAN VACATION

**$100**    WHAT IS THE EIFFEL TOWER?    **$100**

**$200**    WHAT IS PRAGUE?    **$200**

**$300**    WHAT ARE ITALY & VATICAN CITY?    **$300**

**$400**    WHO IS REMBRANDT (VAN RIJN)?    **$400**

**$500**    WHAT IS COPENHAGEN?    **$500**

# JEOPARDY!™

## NOW THAT'S COMEDY

| | | |
|---|---|---|
| IN "TAKE THE MONEY AND RUN", THIS COMEDIAN BUNGLES A BANK ROBBERY BECAUSE NO ONE CAN READ HIS NOTE | **$100** | WHO IS |
| ONE OF THESE DAVID LETTERMAN BITS IS "LEAST POPULAR CANDY BARS"; NO. 4 IS "GOOD 'N' LINTY" | **$200** | WHAT ARE |
| IN AN EARLY ROUTINE, BOB NEWHART INSTRUCTS DRIVERS OF THESE ON PULLING AWAY JUST AS PEOPLE REACH THE DOORS | **$300** | WHAT ARE |
| BUXOM WOMEN LOSING THEIR CLOTHES WAS A STAPLE OF THIS COMIC'S SHOW, ON BRITISH TV UNTIL 1989 | **$400** | WHO IS |
| DANNY THOMAS WAS A MASTER OF THIS "TAKE" IN WHICH HE'D GET STARTLING NEWS WHILE EATING OR DRINKING | **$500** | WHAT IS |

# JEOPARDY!

## NOW THAT'S COMEDY

$100    WHO IS WOODY ALLEN?    $100

$200    WHAT ARE TOP TEN LISTS?    $200

$300    WHAT ARE BUSES?    $300

$400    WHO IS BENNY HILL?    $400

$500    WHAT IS A SPIT TAKE?    $500

# DOUBLE JEOPARDY!

## CANADIAN STUFF, EH?

| | | |
|---|---|---|
| THIS "STAMPEDE" CITY LIES IN THE FOOTHILLS OF THE CANADIAN ROCKIES, SO IT'S NICKNAMED THE "FOOTHILLS CITY" | $200 | WHAT IS |
| PIE-IX, DE L'EGLISE & L'ASSOMPTION ARE STOPS ON THIS CITY'S METRO | $400 | WHAT IS |
| IT'S BEEN CALLED "BRITAIN'S OLDEST COLONY", BUT IT'S CANADA'S "NEW"EST PROVINCE | $600 | WHAT IS |
| LADY SLIPPER DRIVE, A SCENIC ROUTE IN THIS TINY ISLAND PROVINCE, IS NAMED FOR THE PROVINCE'S OFFICIAL FLOWER | $800 | WHAT IS |
| 2 OF THESE LONG-TUSKED WHALES ADORN THE COAT OF ARMS OF CANADA'S NORTHWEST TERRITORIES | $1000 | WHAT ARE |

# DOUBLE JEOPARDY!

## CANADIAN STUFF, EH?

| | |
|---|---|
| **$200** | WHAT IS CALGARY? |
| **$400** | WHAT IS MONTREAL? |
| **$600** | WHAT IS NEWFOUNDLAND? |
| **$800** | WHAT IS PRINCE EDWARD ISLAND? (ACCEPT: P.E.I.) |
| **$1000** | WHAT ARE NARWHALS? |

# DOUBLE JEOPARDY!

## BEAUTY

| | | |
|---|---|---|
| SHORT MASCULINE NICKNAME THAT'S ALSO A WOMEN'S SHORT HAIRSTYLE | **$200** | WHAT IS |
| COSMETIC WHOSE NAME IS SPANISH FOR "MASK" | **$400** | WHAT IS |
| "BECAUSE I'M WORTH IT" IS A CLASSIC SLOGAN OF THIS LINE OF COSMETICS FROM PARIS | **$600** | WHAT IS |
| A COSMETIC USED AS A BASE FOR MAKEUP; PERHAPS THE FORD MODELING AGENCY HAS ITS OWN BRAND | **$800** | WHAT IS |
| FROM LATIN FOR "TO SOFTEN", THIS WORD IS FOUND IN MANY SKIN CARE PRODUCT ADS | **$1000** | WHAT IS |

# DOUBLE JEOPARDY!

## BEAUTY

| | | |
|---|---|---|
| $200 | WHAT IS BOB? | $200 |
| $400 | WHAT IS MASCARA? | $400 |
| $600 | WHAT IS L'OREAL? | $600 |
| $800 | WHAT IS FOUNDATION? | $800 |
| $1000 | WHAT IS EMOLLIENT? | $1000 |

# DOUBLE JEOPARDY!

## SPORTS

| | | |
|---|---|---|
| AFTER 36 SEASONS IN THIS STADIUM NAMED FOR A U.S. SENATOR, THE REDSKINS MOVED TO A NEW FACILITY IN 1997 | **$200** | WHAT IS |
| THIS COACH OF THE NBA'S LAKERS, KNICKS & HEAT IS AUTHOR OF A BOOK CALLED "THE WINNER WITHIN" | **$400** | WHO IS |
| IN 1996, WITH THE OAKLAND A'S, THIS FIRST BASEMAN HIT 52 HOME RUNS—HE WAS JUST WARMING UP | **$600** | WHO IS |
| HE WAS THE INDY 500 ROOKIE OF THE YEAR IN 1965; HIS SON MICHAEL GOT THE HONOR IN 1984 | **$800** | WHO IS |
| ABE MITCHELL IS THE GOLFER DEPICTED ON THIS CUP SOUGHT BY TEAMS FROM THE U.S. & EUROPE | **$1000** | WHAT IS |

# DOUBLE JEOPARDY!

## SPORTS

| | | |
|---|---|---|
| **$200** | WHAT IS RFK STADIUM? | **$200** |
| **$400** | WHO IS PAT RILEY? | **$400** |
| **$600** | WHO IS MARK McGWIRE? | **$600** |
| **$800** | WHO IS MARIO ANDRETTI? | **$800** |
| **$1000** | WHAT IS THE RYDER CUP? | **$1000** |

# DOUBLE JEOPARDY!

## MIDDLE NAMES

| | | |
|---|---|---|
| MIDDLE NAME OF BASEBALL PITCHER LYNN RYAN JR. | **$200** | WHAT IS |
| MIDDLE NAME OF SONGWRITER JAMES McCARTNEY | **$400** | WHAT IS |
| MIDDLE NAME OF DIRECTOR ERNST BERGMAN | **$600** | WHAT IS |
| MIDDLE NAME OF CIVIL RIGHTS LEADER LEROY CLEAVER | **$800** | WHAT IS |
| MIDDLE NAME OF COMMUNICATION THEORIST HERBERT McLUHAN | **$1000** | WHAT IS |

# DOUBLE JEOPARDY!

## MIDDLE NAMES

| | |
|---|---|
| $200 | WHAT IS NOLAN? | $200 |
| $400 | WHAT IS PAUL? | $400 |
| $600 | WHAT IS INGMAR? | $600 |
| $800 | WHAT IS ELDRIDGE? | $800 |
| $1000 | WHAT IS MARSHALL? | $1000 |

# DOUBLE JEOPARDY!

## LOUIS XIV

| | | |
|---|---|---|
| LOUIS' NICKNAME; HE USED THE SYMBOL AS HIS EMBLEM | **$200** | WHAT IS |
| CHARLES DE BATZ, SIEUR D'ARTAGNAN, A SOLDIER IN LOUIS' SERVICE, IS WELL KNOWN BECAUSE OF THIS 1844 NOVEL | **$400** | WHAT IS |
| IT WAS LOUIS' MONEY PIT; ONCE HE STARTED BUILDING THIS ROYAL RESIDENCE IN THE 1660s IT WAS HARD TO STOP | **$600** | WHAT IS |
| AT THIS AGE LOUIS SAID, "TODAY I AM A MAN" & DUMPED HIS MOTHER AS REGENT | **$800** | WHAT IS |
| WANTING THE HUGUENOTS TO CONVERT, LOUIS REVOKED THE EDICT OF THIS IN 1685 | **$1000** | WHAT IS |

# DOUBLE JEOPARDY!

## LOUIS XIV

$200 | WHAT IS THE SUN KING? | $200

$400 | WHAT IS "THE THREE MUSKETEERS"? | $400

$600 | WHAT IS THE PALACE OF VERSAILLES? | $600

$800 | WHAT IS 13? | $800

$1000 | WHAT IS NANTES? | $1000

# DOUBLE JEOPARDY!

## STARTS & ENDS WITH "T"

| | | |
|---|---|---|
| IF YOU NEVER SAY DYE, SAY THIS, A LIGHT DYE FOR THE HAIR | $200 | WHAT IS |
| DINING ACCESSORY USED TO PROTECT THE TABLE FROM A HOT DISH | $400 | WHAT IS |
| ONE TO SEE THE MOVIE "SPEED" IS GOOD; ONE FOR SPEEDING IS BAD | $600 | WHAT IS |
| THIS PROFESSIONAL WILL STUFF YOUR TURKEY...OR YOUR MOOSE, OR YOUR MARLIN | $800 | WHAT IS |
| IT'S AN EXTENDED OUTLINE OF A MOVIE | $1000 | WHAT IS |

# DOUBLE JEOPARDY!

## STARTS & ENDS WITH "T"

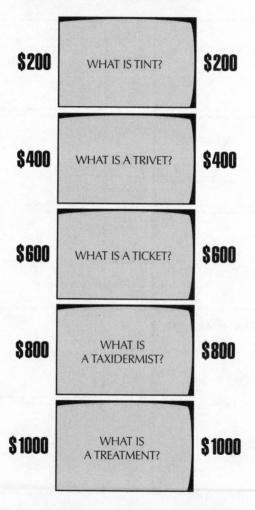

| | | |
|---|---|---|
| **$200** | WHAT IS TINT? | **$200** |
| **$400** | WHAT IS A TRIVET? | **$400** |
| **$600** | WHAT IS A TICKET? | **$600** |
| **$800** | WHAT IS A TAXIDERMIST? | **$800** |
| **$1000** | WHAT IS A TREATMENT? | **$1000** |

# FINAL JEOPARDY!

## 1990s MEDICINE

IN 1998 AN ASPIRIN-ACETAMINOPHEN-CAFFEINE PILL BECAME THE FIRST FDA-APPROVED OVER-THE-COUNTER PILL FOR THIS

WHAT IS

# FINAL JEOPARDY!

## 1990s MEDICINE

WHAT IS MIGRAINE?
(ACCEPT: MIGRAINE
HEADACHES)

# JEOPARDY!

## LITERARY EPICS

| Clue | Value | Response |
|------|-------|----------|
| THIS POET CAST HIMSELF AS THE PROTAGONIST OF THE "DIVINE COMEDY" | $100 | WHO IS |
| THIS TENNYSON WORK BASED ON LEGENDS OF KING ARTHUR FILLS 12 BOOKS | $200 | WHAT ARE |
| PART OF THE ACTION OF THIS OLD ENGLISH POEM TAKES PLACE IN HROTHGAR'S GREAT HALL, HEOROT | $300 | WHAT IS |
| THE "ARGONAUTICA" BY APOLLONIUS OF RHODES TELLS THE STORY OF THE QUEST FOR THIS OBJECT | $400 | WHAT IS |
| THIS ANCIENT MESOPOTAMIAN KING IS THE HERO OF THE EARLIEST KNOWN EPIC POEM | $500 | WHO IS |

# JEOPARDY!

## LITERARY EPICS

| | | |
|---|---|---|
| **$100** | WHO IS DANTE (ALIGHIERI)? | **$100** |
| **$200** | WHAT ARE "IDYLLS OF THE KING"? | **$200** |
| **$300** | WHAT IS "BEOWULF"? | **$300** |
| **$400** | WHAT IS THE GOLDEN FLEECE? | **$400** |
| **$500** | WHO IS GILGAMESH? | **$500** |

# JEOPARDY!™

## BIG IN JAPAN

| | | |
|---|---|---|
| BEAUTY IN THIS BODY PART IS SO VALUED THAT A COMMON INSULT IS "YOUR MOTHER HAS AN OUTIE" | **$100** | WHAT IS |
| THE FILM "A RIVER RUNS THROUGH IT" INSPIRED A JAPANESE CRAZE FOR THIS SPORT | **$200** | WHAT IS |
| THIS TOKYO TRANSIT SYSTEM IS SO POPULAR, "PLATFORM PUSHERS" MAKE SURE EVERYONE GETS ON | **$300** | WHAT IS |
| THE WWII DIARY OF THIS DUTCH JEWISH TEENAGER IS WIDELY READ BY YOUNG JAPANESE GIRLS | **$400** | WHO IS |
| THIS GROUP THAT RECORDED SONGS LIKE "SURRENDER" & "I WANT YOU TO WANT ME" LIVE IN JAPAN REMAINS POPULAR THERE | **$500** | WHAT IS |

# JEOPARDY!

## BIG IN JAPAN

**$100**
WHAT IS THE NAVEL?
(ACCEPT: BELLY
BUTTON)
**$100**

**$200**
WHAT IS
(FLY) FISHING?
(ACCEPT: BASS FISHING)
**$200**

**$300**
WHAT IS
THE SUBWAY?
**$300**

**$400**
WHO IS
ANNE FRANK?
**$400**

**$500**
WHAT IS
CHEAP TRICK?
**$500**

# JEOPARDY!

## TELEVISION

| Clue | Value | Response |
|------|-------|----------|
| THE APARTMENT COMPLEX LOCATED AT 4616 ON THIS TITLE L.A. STREET WAS HOME TO SOME "FOX"Y LADIES | $100 | WHAT IS |
| "PROMISED LAND" WITH GERALD McRANEY WAS SPUN OFF FROM THIS HEAVENLY CBS SERIES | $200 | WHAT IS |
| HE'S PLAYED PETE RYAN, ALEXANDER MUNDY & JONATHAN HART | $300 | WHO IS |
| MANDY PATINKIN LEFT, THEN RETURNED TO THE ROLE OF DR. GEIGER ON THIS DRAMA | $400 | WHAT IS |
| SHE'S BEEN HALF OF "CAGNEY & LACEY" & THE MOTHER OF "JUDGING AMY" | $500 | WHO IS |

# JEOPARDY!

## TELEVISION

| | | |
|---|---|---|
| **$100** | WHAT IS "MELROSE PLACE"? | **$100** |
| **$200** | WHAT IS "TOUCHED BY AN ANGEL"? | **$200** |
| **$300** | WHO IS ROBERT WAGNER? | **$300** |
| **$400** | WHAT IS "CHICAGO HOPE"? | **$400** |
| **$500** | WHO IS TYNE DALY? | **$500** |

110

# JEOPARDY!™

## ANIMALS

| Clue | Value | Response |
|------|-------|----------|
| THE MONKEY-EATING SPECIES OF THIS BIRD LIVES IN THE PHILIPPINES; THE BALD SPECIES LIVES IN THE U.S. | $100 | WHAT IS |
| THIS "RIVER HORSE" CAN WEIGH MORE THAN 8,000 POUNDS | $200 | WHAT IS |
| THE ICHNEUMON IS AN AFRICAN SPECIES OF THIS ANIMAL FAMED FOR ITS SNAKE-FIGHTING ABILITIES | $300 | WHAT IS |
| THESE BIRDS RANGE IN SIZE FROM THE 1-FOOT BLUE TO THE 4-FOOT EMPEROR | $400 | WHAT ARE |
| THESE LIZARDS THAT INCLUDE THE KOMODO DRAGON WOULD BE EFFECTIVE AT PATROLLING THE HALL | $500 | WHAT ARE |

# JEOPARDY!

## ANIMALS

| | |
|---|---|
| **$100** | WHAT IS THE EAGLE? **$100** |
| **$200** | WHAT IS THE HIPPOPOTAMUS? **$200** |
| **$300** | WHAT IS THE MONGOOSE? **$300** |
| **$400** | WHAT ARE PENGUINS? **$400** |
| **$500** | WHAT ARE MONITOR LIZARDS? **$500** |

# JEOPARDY!

## SPENCERS FOR HIRE

| | | |
|---|---|---|
| SPENCER WAS THE MIDDLE NAME OF THIS "LITTLE TRAMP" | **$100** | WHO IS |
| AS SECRETARY OF THIS D.C. INSTITUTION, SPENCER BAIRD BEGAN THE COLLECTION HOUSED IN ITS MUSEUMS | **$200** | WHAT IS |
| THIS ACTOR WHO PLAYED FATHER FLANAGAN IN 1938 ONCE ASPIRED TO THE PRIESTHOOD | **$300** | WHO IS |
| 19th CENTURY DARWINIAN THINKER HERBERT SPENCER IS CREDITED WITH COINING THE PHRASE "SURVIVAL OF" THESE | **$400** | WHO ARE |
| "GIMME SOME LOVIN'" & "I'M A MAN" WERE HITS FOR THIS MAN'S "GROUP" | **$500** | WHO IS |

# JEOPARDY!

## SPENCERS FOR HIRE

$100   WHO IS CHARLIE CHAPLIN?   $100

$200   WHAT IS THE SMITHSONIAN INSTITUTION?   $200

$300   WHO IS SPENCER TRACY?   $300

$400   WHO ARE THE FITTEST?   $400

$500   WHO IS SPENCER DAVIS?   $500

# JEOPARDY!

## "C" OF LOVE

| Clue | Value | Response |
|------|-------|----------|
| THE TITLE OF A 1958 CONNIE FRANCIS SONG CALLS THIS LOVE GOD "STUPID" | **$100** | WHO IS |
| IF YOU DIDN'T SHOW UP FOR A BLIND DATE, YOU HAVE THESE KIND OF "FEET" | **$200** | WHAT ARE |
| FROM AN OLD WORD FOR "CAPE", IT'S AN OLDER PERSON WHO, FOR PROPRIETY'S SAKE, ACCOMPANIES YOUNG UNMARRIEDS | **$300** | WHAT IS |
| THE YOUNGEST DAUGHTER OF KING LEAR, SHE WAS THE ONLY ONE WHO REALLY LOVED HIM | **$400** | WHO IS |
| ITALIAN FOR "WITH LOVE", IT'S THE MUSICAL DIRECTION TO PLAY OR SING LOVINGLY | **$500** | WHAT IS |

# JEOPARDY!

## "C" OF LOVE

| | | |
|---|---|---|
| **$100** | WHO IS CUPID? | **$100** |
| **$200** | WHAT ARE COLD FEET? | **$200** |
| **$300** | WHAT IS A CHAPERONE? | **$300** |
| **$400** | WHO IS CORDELIA? | **$400** |
| **$500** | WHAT IS CON AMORE? | **$500** |

# DOUBLE JEOPARDY!

## AMERICAN HISTORY

| | | |
|---|---|---|
| BRITISH COMMANDER SIR EDWARD PAKENHAM DIED IN THE BATTLE OF THIS CITY, FOUGHT AFTER A TREATY ENDED THE WAR OF 1812 | **$200** | WHAT IS |
| ON MARCH 27, 1964 THIS LARGEST ALASKA CITY WAS HIT BY AN 8.4 EARTHQUAKE | **$400** | WHAT IS |
| IN 1787 ARTHUR ST. CLAIR BECAME THE FIRST GOVERNOR OF THIS VAST "TERRITORY" NORTH OF THE OHIO RIVER | **$600** | WHAT IS |
| ON NOVEMBER 14, 1889 THE NEW YORK WORLD CALLED THIS JOURNALIST'S TRIP "THE LONGEST JOURNEY KNOWN TO MANKIND" | **$800** | WHO IS |
| THIS TRAIL THAT TOOK TEXAS CATTLE TO KANSAS WAS NAMED FOR A TRADER NAMED JESSE | **$1000** | WHAT IS |

# DOUBLE JEOPARDY!

## AMERICAN HISTORY

| $200 | WHAT IS NEW ORLEANS? | $200 |
|---|---|---|
| $400 | WHAT IS ANCHORAGE? | $400 |
| $600 | WHAT IS THE NORTHWEST TERRITORY? | $600 |
| $800 | WHO IS NELLIE BLY? (ACCEPT: ELIZABETH COCHRANE SEAMAN) | $800 |
| $1000 | WHAT IS THE CHISHOLM TRAIL? | $1000 |

# DOUBLE JEOPARDY!

## DOCS

| Clue | Value | Response |
|------|-------|----------|
| ALBERT SABIN, BEST KNOWN FOR HIS ORAL VACCINE FOR THIS, ALSO DEVELOPED A VACCINE FOR DENGUE FEVER | $200 | WHAT IS |
| IN 1967 THIS "BABY AND CHILD CARE" AUTHOR RESIGNED AS A COLLEGE TEACHER TO JOIN THE ANTIWAR MOVEMENT FULL-TIME | $400 | WHO IS |
| MANY AMERICANS CAN GIVE THEIR HEARTFELT THANKS TO THIS HOUSTON SURGEON, THE FIRST TO REPAIR AN ANEURYSM | $600 | WHO IS |
| HANS SELYE PIONEERED THE STUDY OF THIS & WROTE A BOOK ABOUT IT "WITHOUT DISTRESS" | $800 | WHAT IS |
| IN 1778 THIS SMALLPOX VACCINE DEVELOPER WROTE A PAPER ON THE MURDEROUS HABITS OF THE YOUNG CUCKOO BIRD | $1000 | WHO IS |

# DOUBLE JEOPARDY!

## DOCS

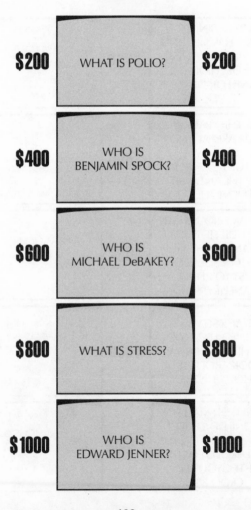

| | | |
|---|---|---|
| **$200** | WHAT IS POLIO? | **$200** |
| **$400** | WHO IS BENJAMIN SPOCK? | **$400** |
| **$600** | WHO IS MICHAEL DeBAKEY? | **$600** |
| **$800** | WHAT IS STRESS? | **$800** |
| **$1000** | WHO IS EDWARD JENNER? | **$1000** |

# DOUBLE JEOPARDY!

## WE, THE JURY

| | | |
|---|---|---|
| IN 1970 THE SUPREME COURT DECLARED THIS STANDARD NUMBER OF JURORS A "HISTORICAL ACCIDENT" | **$200** | WHAT IS |
| WHAT A JURY DOES WHEN IT CAN'T AGREE, OR WHAT IT MAY SENTENCE A MURDERER TO | **$400** | WHAT IS |
| IN A PERSONAL INJURY LAWSUIT, THE JURY MAY CALCULATE BOTH PUNITIVE & COMPENSATORY TYPES OF THESE | **$600** | WHAT ARE |
| THE RIGHT TO HAVE A JURY OF THESE, MEANING ONE'S EQUALS, NOT LORDS, IS MENTIONED IN THE MAGNA CARTA | **$800** | WHAT ARE |
| A LAWYER'S REJECTION OF A PROSPECTIVE JUROR, IT MAY BE "FOR CAUSE" OR "PEREMPTORY" | **$1000** | WHAT IS |

# DOUBLE JEOPARDY!

## WE, THE JURY

**$200**   WHAT IS 12?   **$200**

**$400**   WHAT IS HANG?   **$400**

**$600**   WHAT ARE DAMAGES?   **$600**

**$800**   WHAT ARE (ONE'S) PEERS?   **$800**

**$1000**   WHAT IS A CHALLENGE?   **$1000**

# DOUBLE JEOPARDY!

## FILMS OF THE '70s

| Clue | Value | Response |
|---|---|---|
| WARNER BROS. HAD RIGHTS TO "THE TOWER", FOX HAD RIGHTS TO "THE GLASS INFERNO" & THIS MOVIE WAS THE RESULT | $200 | WHAT IS |
| 14-LETTER WORD COINED TO DESCRIBE FILMS LIKE "SHAFT" & "SUPERFLY" | $400 | WHAT IS |
| IN THIS FILM MARTIN SCORSESE, AS ONE OF ROBERT DE NIRO'S FARES, TALKS ABOUT KILLING HIS WIFE | $600 | WHAT IS |
| LINDSAY WAGNER PLAYED PROFESSOR KINGSFIELD'S DAUGHTER IN THIS 1973 FILM SET AT HARVARD LAW SCHOOL | $800 | WHAT IS |
| A 1975 ROBERT ALTMAN FILM CENTERS ON A MUSIC FESTIVAL & POLITICAL RALLY IN THIS TITLE CITY | $1000 | WHAT IS |

# DOUBLE JEOPARDY!

## FILMS OF THE '70s

| | |
|---|---|
| **$200** | WHAT IS "THE TOWERING INFERNO"? |
| **$400** | WHAT IS BLAXPLOITATION? |
| **$600** | WHAT IS "TAXI DRIVER"? |
| **$800** | WHAT IS "THE PAPER CHASE"? |
| **$1000** | WHAT IS NASHVILLE? |

# DOUBLE JEOPARDY!

## OBSCURE MYTHOLOGY

| | | |
|---|---|---|
| ACCORDING TO AUSTRALIAN MYTH, THIS PHENOMENON SEEN IN THE SKY IS A GIANT SNAKE ARCHING ITS BODY | $200 | WHAT IS |
| HUITZILOPOCHTLI, A GOD OF THESE PEOPLE, WAS SO FIERCE HE KILLED SEVERAL RELATIVES AS SOON AS HE WAS BORN | $400 | WHO ARE |
| GULLINKAMBI IS THE GOLDEN COCK WHO AROUSES THE EINHER-JAR IN THIS NORSE "HALL OF THE SLAIN" | $600 | WHAT IS |
| THE CHINESE GODDESS CH'ANG-O WAS TURNED INTO A TOAD, & HER SHADOW MAY BE SEEN ON THIS HEAVENLY BODY | $800 | WHAT IS |
| THE EGYPTIAN GODDESS NEITH IS OFTEN DEPICTED HOLDING A SCEPTER & THIS SYMBOL OF LIFE | $1000 | WHAT IS |

# DOUBLE JEOPARDY!

## OBSCURE MYTHOLOGY

$200    WHAT IS THE RAINBOW?    $200

$400    WHO ARE THE AZTECS?    $400

$600    WHAT IS VALHALLA?    $600

$800    WHAT IS THE MOON?    $800

$1000    WHAT IS AN ANKH?    $1000

# DOUBLE JEOPARDY!

## CELEBRITY RHYME TIME

| | | |
|---|---|---|
| SHIELDS' CHEFS | **$200** | WHAT ARE |
| MIDLER'S PLANES | **$400** | WHAT ARE |
| BRAD'S FANCY HOTEL | **$600** | WHAT IS |
| THE CONTENTS OF MIA'S QUIVER | **$800** | WHAT ARE |
| TWYLA'S STRINGED INSTRUMENTS | **$1000** | WHAT ARE |

# DOUBLE JEOPARDY!

## CELEBRITY RHYME TIME

| | | |
|---|---|---|
| **$200** | WHAT ARE BROOKE'S COOKS? | **$200** |
| **$400** | WHAT ARE BETTE'S JETS? | **$400** |
| **$600** | WHAT IS PITT'S RITZ? | **$600** |
| **$800** | WHAT ARE FARROW'S ARROWS? | **$800** |
| **$1000** | WHAT ARE THARP'S HARPS? | **$1000** |

## WORLD CITIES

IN 1634 A SPANISH ROYAL
DECREE RECOGNIZED IT AS
THE "KEY TO THE NEW
WORLD AND THE BULWARK
OF THE WEST INDIES"

WHAT IS

# FINAL JEOPARDY!
## WORLD CITIES

WHAT IS HAVANA (CUBA)?

# JEOPARDY!

## THE FAB (18)50s

| | | |
|---|---|---|
| ON JUNE 16, 1858 LINCOLN DECLARED THAT ONE OF THESE "DIVIDED AGAINST ITSELF CANNOT STAND" | $100 | WHAT IS |
| IN 1852 THE ALBANY EVENING JOURNAL COINED THIS WORD TO BE USED INSTEAD OF "TELEGRAPHIC DISPATCH" | $200 | WHAT IS |
| DICKENS TACKLED THE FRENCH REVOLUTION IN THIS 1859 WORK | $300 | WHAT IS |
| THE 1857 SUPREME COURT DECISION CONCERNING THIS ONETIME SLAVE PERMITTED SLAVERY IN ALL U.S. TERRITORIES | $400 | WHO IS |
| THE TREATY OF PARIS OF 1856 ENDING THIS WAR FORCED RUSSIA TO GIVE UP THE MOUTH OF THE DANUBE TO TURKEY | $500 | WHAT IS |

# JEOPARDY!

## THE FAB (18)50s

| | | |
|---|---|---|
| **$100** | WHAT IS A HOUSE? | **$100** |
| **$200** | WHAT IS TELEGRAM? | **$200** |
| **$300** | WHAT IS "A TALE OF TWO CITIES"? | **$300** |
| **$400** | WHO IS DRED SCOTT? | **$400** |
| **$500** | WHAT IS THE CRIMEAN WAR? | **$500** |

# JEOPARDY!

## SCHOOL DAZE

| | | |
|---|---|---|
| IN 1997 EVANSTON, ILLINOIS BRIEFLY BANNED THESE 15-MINUTE BREAKS IN ITS ELEMENTARY SCHOOLS | **$100** | WHAT ARE |
| IN 1993 NYC'S SCHOOLS OPENED 11 DAYS LATE AFTER EMERGENCY INSPECTION OF THIS BUILDING MATERIAL | **$200** | WHAT IS |
| AS THEIR NAME INDICATES, THESE SCHOOLS WERE ESTABLISHED TO "ATTRACT" STUDENTS FROM ACROSS THE CITY | **$300** | WHAT ARE |
| FROM LATIN FOR "SUMMON", THEY'RE CERTIFICATES GIVING PUBLIC FUNDS TO SEND KIDS TO PRIVATE SCHOOLS | **$400** | WHAT ARE |
| "CATHOLIC" MEANS BROADMINDED, BUT CATHOLIC SCHOOLS ARE THIS TYPE, WHICH ALSO MEANS NARROWMINDED | **$500** | WHAT IS |

# JEOPARDY!

## SCHOOL DAZE

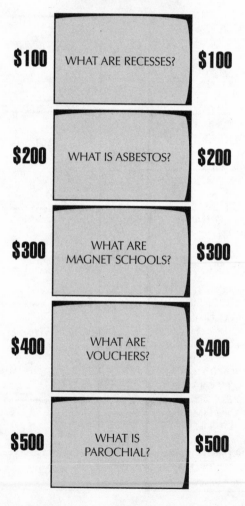

**$100**    WHAT ARE RECESSES?    **$100**

**$200**    WHAT IS ASBESTOS?    **$200**

**$300**    WHAT ARE MAGNET SCHOOLS?    **$300**

**$400**    WHAT ARE VOUCHERS?    **$400**

**$500**    WHAT IS PAROCHIAL?    **$500**

# JEOPARDY!

## MOM'S THE WORD

| Clue | Value | Response |
|------|-------|----------|
| ETHEL SKAKEL MARRIED THIS POLITICIAN IN 1950 & BORE HIM 11 CHILDREN, THE LAST AFTER HIS DEATH | **$100** | WHO IS |
| IN 1997 A 63-YEAR-OLD CALIFORNIA WOMAN MADE HEADLINES BY SETTING THIS GUINNESS RECORD | **$200** | WHAT IS |
| MIRIAM WEINSTEIN & HER HUSBAND MAX PROVIDED THIS NAME FOR A FILM COMPANY FOUNDED BY THEIR SONS IN 1980 | **$300** | WHAT IS |
| IN 1997 BRENDA BARNES LEFT THE UPPER ECHELONS OF THIS SODA COMPANY TO BE WITH GENERATION NEXT, HER KIDS | **$400** | WHAT IS |
| SHE'S GWYNETH PALTROW'S MOM, & SHE PLAYED JONATHAN SILVERMAN'S MOM IN "BRIGHTON BEACH MEMOIRS" | **$500** | WHO IS |

# JEOPARDY!

## MOM'S THE WORD

| | | |
|---|---|---|
| **$100** | WHO IS ROBERT F. KENNEDY? | **$100** |
| **$200** | WHAT IS OLDEST (NEW) MOTHER? | **$200** |
| **$300** | WHAT IS MIRAMAX? | **$300** |
| **$400** | WHAT IS PEPSI-COLA (NORTH AMERICA)? | **$400** |
| **$500** | WHO IS BLYTHE DANNER? | **$500** |

# JEOPARDY!

## INDIANAGRAMS

| | | |
|---|---|---|
| GRAY | **$100** | WHAT IS |
| I SAIL IN A POND | **$200** | WHAT IS |
| BEST HOUND | **$300** | WHAT IS |
| VILLA SEVEN | **$400** | WHAT IS |
| RUE THE RATE | **$500** | WHAT IS |

# JEOPARDY!

## INDIANAGRAMS

| | | |
|---|---|---|
| **$100** | WHAT IS GARY? | **$100** |
| **$200** | WHAT IS INDIANAPOLIS? | **$200** |
| **$300** | WHAT IS SOUTH BEND? | **$300** |
| **$400** | WHAT IS EVANSVILLE? | **$400** |
| **$500** | WHAT IS TERRE HAUTE? | **$500** |

# JEOPARDY!™

## THE UNITED NATIONS

| | | |
|---|---|---|
| IN 1974 THIS PLO LEADER ADDRESSED THE GENERAL ASSEMBLY WEARING A GUN & HOLSTER | **$100** | WHO IS |
| IN 1980 THE U.N. PASSED A RESOLUTION DEMANDING THE SOVIET UNION WITH-DRAW FROM THIS COUNTRY | **$200** | WHAT IS |
| IN 1950 THIS 39-STORY BUILDING WAS COMPLETED NEAR THE EAST RIVER | **$300** | WHAT IS |
| IN 1961 A NEW U.N. LIBRARY WAS DEDICATED & NAMED FOR THIS SWEDISH SECRETARY-GENERAL | **$400** | WHO IS |
| THIS BLACK AMERICAN HELPED WRITE THE U.N. CHARTER & WENT ON TO WIN A NOBEL PEACE PRIZE | **$500** | WHO IS |

# JEOPARDY!

## THE UNITED NATIONS

| | | |
|---|---|---|
| $100 | WHO IS YASIR ARAFAT? | $100 |
| $200 | WHAT IS AFGHANISTAN? | $200 |
| $300 | WHAT IS THE SECRETARIAT? | $300 |
| $400 | WHO IS DAG HAMMARSKJOLD? | $400 |
| $500 | WHO IS RALPH BUNCHE? | $500 |

# JEOPARDY!

## UNDER THE COVERS

| Clue | Value | Response |
|------|-------|----------|
| SIOUXSIE & THE BANSHEES' COVER VERSION OF THIS GROUP'S "DEAR PRUDENCE" HIT NO. 3 IN THE U.K. | **$100** | WHO ARE |
| THIS DEXYS MIDNIGHT RUNNERS NO. 1 HIT WAS SUCCESSFULLY COVERED BY SKA BAND SAVE FERRIS | **$200** | WHAT IS |
| IN 1996 THE FUGEES UPDATED HER 1973 HIT "KILLING ME SOFTLY" | **$300** | WHO IS |
| THIS WELSH POP LEGEND TEAMED WITH THE ART OF NOISE TO HAVE A HIT WITH PRINCE'S SONG "KISS" | **$400** | WHO IS |
| DOLLY PARTON & 10,000 MANIACS HAVE RIDDEN TO SUCCESS WITH VERSIONS OF THIS CAT STEVENS SONG | **$500** | WHAT IS |

# JEOPARDY!

## UNDER THE COVERS

| | | |
|---|---|---|
| $100 | WHO ARE THE BEATLES? | $100 |
| $200 | WHAT IS "COME ON EILEEN"? | $200 |
| $300 | WHO IS ROBERTA FLACK? | $300 |
| $400 | WHO IS TOM JONES? | $400 |
| $500 | WHAT IS "PEACE TRAIN"? | $500 |

# DOUBLE JEOPARDY!

## FAMOUS FRENCHMEN

| | | |
|---|---|---|
| THIS MARINE EXPLORER WON AN OSCAR FOR THE 1956 DOCUMENTARY "THE SILENT WORLD" | **$200** | WHO IS |
| IN 1619 THIS MATH WHIZ COULD HAVE SAID, "I THINK, THEREFORE I AM JOINING THE DUKE OF BAVARIA'S ARMY" | **$400** | WHO IS |
| THIS CARDINAL, "THE RED EMINENCE", MADE HIS ENEMIES SEE RED, SO HE WAS BANISHED IN 1617 | **$600** | WHO IS |
| PLAYWRIGHT JEAN-BAPTISTE POQUELIN BEGAN USING THIS 1-WORD STAGE NAME IN THE 1640S | **$800** | WHAT IS |
| THIS DIRECTOR'S FILMS INCLUDE "JULES AND JIM" & THE AUTOBIOGRAPHICAL "THE 400 BLOWS" | **$1000** | WHO IS |

# DOUBLE JEOPARDY!

## FAMOUS FRENCHMEN

$200 — WHO IS JACQUES (-YVES) COUSTEAU? — $200

$400 — WHO IS RENE DESCARTES? — $400

$600 — WHO IS CARDINAL RICHELIEU? — $600

$800 — WHAT IS MOLIERE? — $800

$1000 — WHO IS FRANCOIS TRUFFAUT? — $1000

# DOUBLE JEOPARDY!

## MUSICAL INSTRUMENTS

| | | |
|---|---|---|
| THE MOUTHPIECE OF AN OBOE CONTAINS A DOUBLE ONE | **$200** | WHAT IS |
| A FLAMENCO DANCER SHOULD ALSO BE ACCOMPLISHED ON THESE PERCUSSION INSTRUMENTS | **$400** | WHAT ARE |
| HEARD IN STRING QUARTETS, IT'S 1-3 INCHES LONGER THAN A VIOLIN | **$600** | WHAT IS |
| A TYPE OF TRAP FOR ANIMALS, OR A TYPE OF SIDE DRUM | **$800** | WHAT IS |
| POPULARIZED BY LIONEL HAMPTON, YOU HAVE TO PLUG IT IN FIRST | **$1000** | WHAT IS |

# DOUBLE JEOPARDY!

## MUSICAL INSTRUMENTS

| | | |
|---|---|---|
| **$200** | WHAT IS A REED? | **$200** |
| **$400** | WHAT ARE CASTANETS? | **$400** |
| **$600** | WHAT IS A VIOLA? | **$600** |
| **$800** | WHAT IS A SNARE? | **$800** |
| **$1000** | WHAT IS THE VIBRAPHONE? (ACCEPT: VIBES) | **$1000** |

# DOUBLE JEOPARDY!

## BASEBALL

| Clue | Value | Response |
|---|---|---|
| THE AWARD FOR OUTSTANDING PITCHER IN EACH LEAGUE IS NAMED FOR THIS OLD-TIME 500-GAME WINNER | $200 | WHO IS |
| THIS SEATTLE MARINER WAS NAMED MVP OF THE 1992 ALL-STAR GAME; HIS FATHER WON THE AWARD IN 1980 | $400 | WHO IS |
| THIS CENTER FIELDER HIT A CAREER RECORD 18 WORLD SERIES HOME RUNS—3 MORE THAN BABE RUTH | $600 | WHO IS |
| IN 1930 HACK WILSON SET A LONG-STANDING RECORD WITH 190 OF THESE | $800 | WHAT ARE |
| THIS YANKEE RELIEF PITCHER WAS MVP OF THE 1999 WORLD SERIES | $1000 | WHO IS |

# DOUBLE JEOPARDY!

## BASEBALL

$200 — WHO IS CY YOUNG? — $200

$400 — WHO IS KEN GRIFFEY JR.? — $400

$600 — WHO IS MICKEY MANTLE? — $600

$800 — WHAT ARE RBIs? (ACCEPT: RUNS BATTED IN) — $800

$1000 — WHO IS MARIANO RIVERA? — $1000

# DOUBLE JEOPARDY!

## THEY MIGHT BE GIANTS

| Clue | Value | Response |
|---|---|---|
| THIS TOWERING PHILISTINE STOOD 6 CUBITS & A SPAN, EQUAL TO 9'9" | $200 | WHO IS |
| THIS 7'1", 315-POUND CENTER JOINED THE LAKERS FROM THE MAGIC IN 1996 | $400 | WHO IS |
| AN ANCIENT WONDER, THIS SYMBOL OF LARGENESS STOOD AT THE HARBOR OF RHODES | $600 | WHAT IS |
| THIS "GIANT" OCEAN DWELLER HAS THE LARGEST EYES OF ANY CREATURE | $800 | WHAT IS |
| IN THE WORKS OF RABELAIS, HE WAS GARGANTUA'S SON | $1000 | WHO IS |

149

# DOUBLE JEOPARDY!

## THEY MIGHT BE GIANTS

$200 — WHO IS GOLIATH? — $200

$400 — WHO IS SHAQUILLE O'NEAL? — $400

$600 — WHAT IS THE COLOSSUS (OF RHODES)? — $600

$800 — WHAT IS THE (GIANT) SQUID? — $800

$1000 — WHO IS PANTAGRUEL? — $1000

# DOUBLE JEOPARDY!

## ANCIENT TRAVEL GUIDE

| | | |
|---|---|---|
| VISIT HERE & ENJOY MEDITERRANEAN CUISINE, BEAUTIFUL WOMEN & A HUGE WOODEN HORSE DONATED BY THE GREEKS | **$200** | WHAT IS |
| NO BULL, CRETE WILL A-MAZE YOU AS YOU WANDER THROUGH THE LABYRINTH, THIS CREATURE'S LAIR | **$400** | WHAT IS |
| LUSCIOUS GARDENS HANGING FOR YOUR PLEASURE AWAIT YOU IN THIS ANCIENT CITY ON THE EUPHRATES | **$600** | WHAT IS |
| JOIN US IN THIS AFRICAN HOT SPOT & WE'LL SUPPLY ELEPHANTS & A TOUR OF HANNIBAL'S BIRTHPLACE | **$800** | WHAT IS |
| BARREN ACCOMMODATIONS, BUT PLENTY OF EXERCISE & MILITARY DRILL IN THIS CAPITAL OF LACONIA | **$1000** | WHAT IS |

# DOUBLE JEOPARDY!

## ANCIENT TRAVEL GUIDE

$200 — WHAT IS TROY? — $200

$400 — WHAT IS THE MINOTAUR? — $400

$600 — WHAT IS BABYLON? — $600

$800 — WHAT IS CARTHAGE? — $800

$1000 — WHAT IS SPARTA? (ACCEPT: LACEDAEMON) — $1000

# DOUBLE JEOPARDY!

## PROVERBS

| | | |
|---|---|---|
| IT "CATCHES THE WORM" | **$200** | WHAT IS |
| THERE'S NOT ONLY ONE "TO EVERY RULE", IT ALSO "PROVES THE RULE" | **$400** | WHAT IS |
| PROVERBIALLY, "YOU CAN LEAD A HORSE TO WATER, BUT YOU CAN'T" DO THIS | **$600** | WHAT IS |
| GEORGE BERNARD SHAW WAS THE FIRST TO OBSERVE THAT "HE WHO CAN DOES; HE WHO CANNOT" DOES THIS | **$800** | WHAT IS |
| THE SAYING "THERE IS NOTHING NEW UNDER THE SUN" IS A VARIATION OF A PROVERB IN THIS OLD TESTAMENT BOOK | **$1000** | WHAT IS |

# DOUBLE JEOPARDY!

## PROVERBS

$200　WHAT IS THE EARLY BIRD?　$200

$400　WHAT IS (THE) EXCEPTION?　$400

$600　WHAT IS "MAKE HIM DRINK"?　$600

$800　WHAT IS TEACHES?　$800

$1000　WHAT IS ECCLESIASTES?　$1000

154

# FINAL JEOPARDY!

## 1990s BESTSELLERS

IN 1998, 35 YEARS AFTER
HER DEATH, SHE WAS THE
SUBJECT OF A NEW
COLLECTION OF POEMS
BY HER HUSBAND

WHO IS

# FINAL JEOPARDY!

## 1990s BESTSELLERS

WHO IS SYLVIA PLATH?

# JEOPARDY!™

# A GLADIATOR'S LIFE

| | | |
|---|---|---|
| TRANSLATED FROM LATIN, "GLADIATOR" MEANS A "MAN OF" THIS WEAPON | **$100** | WHAT IS |
| LIKE CERTAIN MOVIE CRITICS, IT'S BELIEVED SPECTATORS DECIDED GLADIATORS' FATE BY DISPLAYING THIS | **$200** | WHAT IS |
| IT'S THE BETTER KNOWN NAME FOR THE FLAVIAN AMPHITHEATER WHERE GLADIATORS FOUGHT | **$300** | WHAT IS |
| THIS 3-PRONGED GLADIATORIAL WEAPON WAS A FAVORITE OF THE GOD NEPTUNE | **$400** | WHAT IS |
| BEFORE HE LED A SLAVE REVOLT IN THE 70s B.C., HE WAS A GLADIATOR IN TRAINING | **$500** | WHO IS |

# JEOPARDY!™

# A GLADIATOR'S LIFE

**$100**  WHAT IS A SWORD?  **$100**

**$200**  WHAT IS THE THUMB?  **$200**

**$300**  WHAT IS THE COLOSSEUM?  **$300**

**$400**  WHAT IS A TRIDENT?  **$400**

**$500**  WHO IS SPARTACUS?  **$500**

# JEOPARDY!

## CONNECTICUTIES

| | | |
|---|---|---|
| IN 1993 THIS FAIRFIELD-BORN ACTRESS STARRED WITH HUSBAND DENNIS QUAID IN "FLESH AND BONE" | **$100** | WHO IS |
| THIS FEMALE STAR OF "THE BIG CHILL" & "DANGEROUS LIAISONS" IS A 12th-GENERATION NEW ENGLANDER | **$200** | WHO IS |
| IN 1933 MARION BERGERON OF WEST HAVEN BECAME THE FIRST & ONLY CONNECTICUTIE CROWNED THIS | **$300** | WHAT IS |
| THIS MAN FROM WATERBURY HAS MADE SOME MOUTHS WATER IN HIS ROLE ON "THE PRACTICE" | **$400** | WHO IS |
| THIS STAR OF TV'S "CHINA BEACH" IS THE HEIRESS TO A TOILET FLUSH VALVE FORTUNE | **$500** | WHO IS |

# JEOPARDY!™

## CONNECTICUTIES

$100    WHO IS MEG RYAN?    $100

$200    WHO IS GLENN CLOSE?    $200

$300    WHAT IS MISS AMERICA?    $300

$400    WHO IS DYLAN McDERMOTT?    $400

$500    WHO IS DANA DELANY?    $500

# JEOPARDY!

## THE PLANE TRUTH

| | | |
|---|---|---|
| WHEN LINDBERGH TOOK THIS PLANE ON A TEST FLIGHT, HE SET A CALIFORNIA-TO-NEW YORK SPEED RECORD | **$100** | WHAT IS |
| HE FLEW HIS FAMOUS GUESTS TO SAN SIMEON IN A VULTEE V1-A | **$200** | WHO IS |
| IN THE LATE '60s BOEING DEVELOPED THE FIRST JUMBO JET & GAVE IT THIS NUMBER | **$300** | WHAT IS |
| IN 1954 THE CONVAIR XFY-1 BECAME THE FIRST PLANE TO MAKE A VTOL—THIS KIND OF TAKE-OFF & LANDING | **$400** | WHAT IS |
| INTRODUCED IN 1944, THIS GERMAN COMPANY'S ME262 WAS THE FIRST JET COMBAT PLANE | **$500** | WHAT IS |

# JEOPARDY!

## THE PLANE TRUTH

| | | |
|---|---|---|
| **$100** | WHAT IS THE SPIRIT OF ST. LOUIS? | **$100** |
| **$200** | WHO IS WILLIAM RANDOLPH HEARST? | **$200** |
| **$300** | WHAT IS 747? | **$300** |
| **$400** | WHAT IS VERTICAL? | **$400** |
| **$500** | WHAT IS MESSERSCHMITT? | **$500** |

# JEOPARDY!™

## GAME SHOW WOMEN

| | | |
|---|---|---|
| BEFORE BEING ON "SALE OF THE CENTURY", SUMMER BARTHOLOMEW PRECEDED VANNA WHITE ON THIS GAME | **$100** | WHAT IS |
| GENA LEE NOLIN OF "THE PRICE IS RIGHT" MOVED ON TO LIFE-GUARD DUTY ON THIS SYNDICATED SERIES | **$200** | WHAT IS |
| SHOW IN COMMON TO JENNY McCARTHY & CARMEN ELECTRA | **$300** | WHAT IS |
| MARK GOODSON'S DAUGHTER MARJORIE WAS A MODEL ON THE "CLASSIC" VERSION OF THIS GAME | **$400** | WHAT IS |
| KC WINKLER, BECKY PRICE & RUTA LEE APPEARED ON VARIOUS VERSIONS OF THIS DICE GAME | **$500** | WHAT IS |

# JEOPARDY!™

## GAME SHOW WOMEN

**$100** — WHAT IS "WHEEL OF FORTUNE"? — **$100**

**$200** — WHAT IS "BAYWATCH"? — **$200**

**$300** — WHAT IS "SINGLED OUT"? — **$300**

**$400** — WHAT IS "CONCENTRATION"? — **$400**

**$500** — WHAT IS "HIGH ROLLERS"? — **$500**

# JEOPARDY!

## EXPLORATION

| | | |
|---|---|---|
| THE FAMOUS GREETING "DR. LIVINGSTONE, I PRESUME?" IS ATTRIBUTED TO HIM | **$100** | WHO IS |
| A CITY IN WHAT IS NOW THIS STATE WAS NAMED TO HONOR JULIEN DUBUQUE, 23 YEARS AFTER HIS DEATH | **$200** | WHAT IS |
| THIS MAN, WHOSE EXPEDITION WAS SECOND TO THE SOUTH POLE, JOINED THE ROYAL NAVY IN 1880, THE YEAR HE TURNED 12 | **$300** | WHO IS |
| IN 1498 THIS PORTUGUESE EXPLORER RECRUITED A PILOT IN EAST AFRICA TO HELP HIM FIND INDIA | **$400** | WHO IS |
| GONZALO JIMENEZ DE QUESADA FOUNDED BOGOTA BETWEEN 2 TRIPS TO FIND THIS MYTHICAL GOLDEN CITY | **$500** | WHAT IS |

# JEOPARDY!

## EXPLORATION

| | | |
|:---:|:---:|:---:|
| **$100** | WHO IS HENRY MORTON STANLEY? | **$100** |
| **$200** | WHAT IS IOWA? | **$200** |
| **$300** | WHO IS ROBERT F. SCOTT? | **$300** |
| **$400** | WHO IS VASCO DA GAMA? | **$400** |
| **$500** | WHAT IS EL DORADO? | **$500** |

# JEOPARDY!™

# THE APOSTROPHE STANDS FOR...

| | | |
|---|---|---|
| IN THE WORD WOULDN'T | **$100** | WHAT IS |
| IN THE WORD DANCIN' | **$200** | WHAT IS |
| IN THE WORD YOU'VE | **$300** | WHAT IS |
| IN THE WORD O'ER | **$400** | WHAT IS |
| IN THE WORD 'TWIXT | **$500** | WHAT IS |

# JEOPARDY!

# THE APOSTROPHE STANDS FOR ...

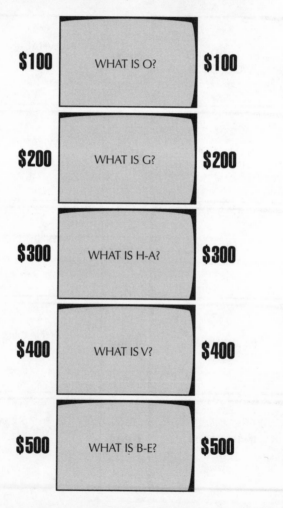

$100     WHAT IS O?     $100

$200     WHAT IS G?     $200

$300     WHAT IS H-A?     $300

$400     WHAT IS V?     $400

$500     WHAT IS B-E?     $500

168

# DOUBLE JEOPARDY!

## SHORT STORY WRITERS

| | | |
|---|---|---|
| IT'S THOUGHT THAT THE "GIFT OF THE MAGI" AUTHOR TOOK THIS PEN NAME PARTLY FROM A PRISON GUARD | **$200** | WHO IS |
| THIS RUSSIAN WROTE CLASSIC SHORT STORIES LIKE "OF LOVE" AS WELL AS CLASSIC PLAYS LIKE "THE CHERRY ORCHARD" | **$400** | WHO IS |
| "THE CELESTIAL RAILROAD" FROM HIS "TWICE-TOLD TALES" IS A PARODY OF JOHN BUNYAN'S WORKS | **$600** | WHO IS |
| SUNNYSIDE, THE OLD DUTCH HOUSE HE REMODELED IN TARRYTOWN, N.Y., WAS MADE A PUBLIC SHRINE IN 1947 | **$800** | WHO IS |
| LATE AMERICAN WHOSE TERSE STYLE IS SEEN IN COLLECTIONS LIKE "WHAT WE TALK ABOUT WHEN WE TALK ABOUT LOVE" | **$1000** | WHO IS |

# DOUBLE JEOPARDY!

## SHORT STORY WRITERS

| $200 | WHO IS O. HENRY? (ACCEPT: WILLIAM SIDNEY PORTER) | $200 |
|---|---|---|
| $400 | WHO IS ANTON CHEKHOV? | $400 |
| $600 | WHO IS NATHANIEL HAWTHORNE? | $600 |
| $800 | WHO IS WASHINGTON IRVING? | $800 |
| $1000 | WHO IS RAYMOND CARVER? | $1000 |

# DOUBLE JEOPARDY!

## FURNITURE

| | | |
|---|---|---|
| OFTEN PART OF THE FRAME, IT'S THE PANEL AT THE PILLOWED END OF A BED | **$200** | WHAT IS |
| A HOME WORKMAN'S HOLDS TOOLS; A BALLPARK'S HOLDS THE HOME TEAM | **$400** | WHAT IS |
| NAMED FOR ITS INVENTOR, THIS BED THAT SWINGS UP INTO A WALL CLOSET WAS A STAPLE OF SILENT SLAPSTICK COMEDY | **$600** | WHAT IS |
| ONCE PAINTED OVER IN EARLY PINE FURNITURE, THESE FLAWS IN THE WOOD GRAIN ARE NOW USED FOR DECORATIVE EFFECT | **$800** | WHAT ARE |
| DUNCAN PHYFE WORKED IN THIS 1780-1830 PERIOD OF AMERICAN FURNITURE, BUT DIDN'T MAKE A "CASE" OF IT | **$1000** | WHAT IS |

# DOUBLE JEOPARDY!

## FURNITURE

| | | |
|---|---|---|
| **$200** | WHAT IS A HEADBOARD? | **$200** |
| **$400** | WHAT IS A BENCH? | **$400** |
| **$600** | WHAT IS THE MURPHY BED? | **$600** |
| **$800** | WHAT ARE KNOTS? | **$800** |
| **$1000** | WHAT IS FEDERAL? | **$1000** |

# DOUBLE JEOPARDY!

## 1980s FILM FACTS

| Clue | Value | Response |
|------|-------|----------|
| SCREENWRITERS LOWELL GANZ & BABALOO MANDEL HOOKED AUDIENCES WITH THIS HANKS-HANNAH MERMAID FILM | $200 | WHAT IS |
| AS ELIOT NESS, KEVIN COSTNER CLEANED UP THE MESS IN CHICAGO IN THIS 1987 FILM | $400 | WHAT IS |
| HE TOOK HOME AN OSCAR FOR PLAYING THE AUTISTIC RAYMOND IN A 1988 FILM | $600 | WHO IS |
| ROBIN WILLIAMS SAILED INTO MOVIE STARDOM AS THIS TITLE CHARACTER OPPOSITE SHELLEY DUVALL AS OLIVE OYL | $800 | WHAT IS |
| THIS OFFBEAT DIRECTOR CAST HIMSELF AS A NUTTY PSYCHIATRIST IN HIS OWN FILM "HAIRSPRAY" | $1000 | WHO IS |

# DOUBLE JEOPARDY!™

## 1980s FILM FACTS

**$200** — WHAT IS "SPLASH"? — **$200**

**$400** — WHAT IS "THE UNTOUCHABLES"? — **$400**

**$600** — WHO IS DUSTIN HOFFMAN? — **$600**

**$800** — WHAT IS POPEYE? — **$800**

**$1000** — WHO IS JOHN WATERS? — **$1000**

# DOUBLE JEOPARDY!

## WIINSTON CHURCHILL

| | | |
|---|---|---|
| EXCEPT FOR 2 YEARS, CHURCHILL SERVED IN THIS "HOUSE" FROM 1900 TO HIS 1964 RESIGNATION | **$200** | WHAT IS |
| THE "FEW" IN WINSTON'S QUOTE, "NEVER IN THE FIELD OF HUMAN CONFLICT WAS SO MUCH OWED BY SO MANY TO SO FEW" | **$400** | WHAT IS |
| CHURCHILL'S MOTHER, BORN JENNIE JEROME, WAS A NATIVE OF THIS COUNTRY | **$600** | WHAT IS |
| CHURCHILL DECLARED THAT AS PRIME MINISTER HE HAD "NOTHING TO OFFER BUT BLOOD, TOIL" & THESE 2 FLUIDS | **$800** | WHAT ARE |
| CHURCHILL WAS DESCENDED FROM JOHN CHURCHILL, THE FIRST DUKE OF THIS | **$1000** | WHAT IS |

# DOUBLE JEOPARDY!

## WIINSTON CHURCHILL

| | | |
|---|---|---|
| **$200** | WHAT IS THE HOUSE OF COMMONS? | **$200** |
| **$400** | WHAT IS THE RAF? (ACCEPT: ROYAL AIR FORCE) | **$400** |
| **$600** | WHAT IS THE UNITED STATES? | **$600** |
| **$800** | WHAT ARE TEARS & SWEAT? | **$800** |
| **$1000** | WHAT IS MARLBOROUGH? | **$1000** |

# DOUBLE JEOPARDY!

## GREEK LETTERS

| Clue | Value | Response |
|------|-------|----------|
| GREEK LETTER YOU NEED TO KNOW TO FIGURE OUT THE AREA OF A CIRCLE | $200 | WHAT IS |
| THIS FOURTH GREEK LETTER IS IN THE TITLE OF HELEN REDDY'S SECOND NO. 1 HIT | $400 | WHAT IS |
| IT'S THE FINAL NAME IN WATCH BRANDS | $600 | WHAT IS |
| COMPUTER GAMES & PROGRAMS UNDERGO THIS TEST PERIOD TO WORK OUT BUGS BEFORE THEIR FINAL RETAIL RELEASE | $800 | WHAT IS |
| EXPLORE AMERICAN SAMOA & YOU'LL COME ACROSS THIS ISLAND THAT'LL SUIT YOU TO A "T" | $1000 | WHAT IS |

# DOUBLE JEOPARDY!

## GREEK LETTERS

| | | |
|---|---|---|
| **$200** | WHAT IS PI? | **$200** |
| **$400** | WHAT IS DELTA? | **$400** |
| **$600** | WHAT IS OMEGA? | **$600** |
| **$800** | WHAT IS BETA (TESTING)? | **$800** |
| **$1000** | WHAT IS TAU? | **$1000** |

# DOUBLE JEOPARDY!

## GIVE IT A MYTH

| | | |
|---|---|---|
| THIS RULER WITH A PLANETARY NAME RARELY, IF EVER, LEAVES HIS DOMAIN, THE UNDERWORLD | **$200** | WHO IS |
| PERSEUS PROVED THIS GORGON WASN'T IMMORTAL | **$400** | WHO IS |
| ADD ONE MORE LETTER TO EOS & YOU'LL GET THIS GOD OF LOVE | **$600** | WHO IS |
| THE GODDESSES APHRODITE & PERSE-PHONE BOTH LOVED THIS YOUTH WHOSE NAME IS APPLIED TO ANY HANDSOME MAN | **$800** | WHO IS |
| YOU COULD SAY THIS KING OF EPHRYA HAD QUITE ENOUGH ROLLING ROCK | **$1000** | WHO IS |

# DOUBLE JEOPARDY!

## GIVE IT A MYTH

$200    WHO IS PLUTO?    $200

$400    WHO IS MEDUSA?    $400

$600    WHO IS EROS?    $600

$800    WHO IS ADONIS?    $800

$1000    WHO IS SISYPHUS?    $1000

# FINAL JEOPARDY!

## SINGERS

HE FIRST RECORDED IN 1939, "RETIRED" IN 1971, RETURNED & HAD A TOP 10 ALBUM IN 1993

WHO IS

# FINAL JEOPARDY!

## SINGERS

WHO IS FRANK SINATRA?

# JEOPARDY!™

## HOOKED ON PHOENIX

| | | |
|---|---|---|
| PERHAPS THIS TEAM'S GREATEST GAME EVER WAS A TRIPLE-OVERTIME LOSS TO THE CELTICS IN THE 1976 FINALS | **$100** | WHO ARE |
| THE NAME OF THE RIVER THAT FLOWS THROUGH PHOENIX, IT'S ALSO FOUND IN THE NAME OF A UTAH LAKE | **$200** | WHAT IS |
| PHOENIX' FIREFIGHTING MUSEUM ISN'T CALLED THE HALL OF FAME BUT THE HALL OF THIS | **$300** | WHAT IS |
| THE ARIZONA BILTMORE WAS INSPIRED BY THE DESIGNS OF THIS MAN WHO LIVED & WORKED AT NEARBY TALIESIN WEST | **$400** | WHO IS |
| BY GUM, THE MANSION BUILT BY THIS CHEWING GUM MOGUL IS A NATIONAL HISTORIC LANDMARK | **$500** | WHO IS |

# JEOPARDY!

## HOOKED ON PHOENIX

$100    WHO ARE THE (PHOENIX) SUNS?    $100

$200    WHAT IS SALT (RIVER)?    $200

$300    WHAT IS (THE HALL OF) FLAME?    $300

$400    WHO IS FRANK LLOYD WRIGHT?    $400

$500    WHO IS WILLIAM WRIGLEY (JR.)?    $500

# JEOPARDY!

## THE '60s

| | | |
|---|---|---|
| THIS CITY'S KING'S ROAD & CARNABY STREET WERE HOT SPOTS OF '60s FASHION | **$100** | WHAT IS |
| MOVIE RATING GIVEN "THE KILLING OF SISTER GEORGE" IN 1968 & "MIDNIGHT COWBOY" IN 1969 | **$200** | WHAT IS |
| THIS COUPLE, WHO APPEARED NUDE ON THEIR 1968 RECORD COVER, WED IN 1969 | **$300** | WHO ARE |
| POLICE WARNINGS STEM FROM THE 1966 SUPREME COURT CASE OF THIS MAN V. ARIZONA | **$400** | WHO IS |
| IT TOOK 18 DAYS TO REPLACE THIS LATE POPE IN 1963 | **$500** | WHO IS |

# JEOPARDY!

## THE '60s

**$100**    WHAT IS LONDON?    **$100**

**$200**    WHAT IS X?    **$200**

**$300**    WHO ARE JOHN LENNON & YOKO ONO?    **$300**

**$400**    WHO IS ERNESTO MIRANDA?    **$400**

**$500**    WHO IS JOHN XXIII?    **$500**

# JEOPARDY!

## GOOD DEEDS

| | | |
|---|---|---|
| IN 1982 LENNY SKUTNICK RESCUED A PASSENGER ON A CRASHED 737 FROM THIS D.C. RIVER | **$100** | WHAT IS |
| FITTINGLY, CNN BROKE THE NEWS IN 1997 WHEN THIS MAN DECIDED TO GIVE $1 BILLION TO THE U.N. | **$200** | WHO IS |
| JODY WILLIAMS WON A 1997 NOBEL PEACE PRIZE FOR HER EFFORTS TO BAN THESE WEAPONS | **$300** | WHAT ARE |
| IN 1997, 5 DECADES LATE, 7 BLACK SOLDIERS RECEIVED THIS HIGHEST AWARD FOR BRAVERY DURING WWII | **$400** | WHAT IS |
| JAPANESE CONSUL CHIUNE SUGIHARA, WHO SAVED HUN-DREDS OF JEWS IN WWII, BEARS THE TITLE "RIGHTEOUS" THIS | **$500** | WHAT IS |

# JEOPARDY!

## GOOD DEEDS

**$100** WHAT IS THE POTOMAC? **$100**

**$200** WHO IS TED TURNER? **$200**

**$300** WHAT ARE LANDMINES? **$300**

**$400** WHAT IS THE (CONGRESSIONAL) MEDAL OF HONOR? **$400**

**$500** WHAT IS GENTILE? (ACCEPT: AMONG THE NATIONS) **$500**

# JEOPARDY!

## MEL BROOKS MOVIES

| Clue | Value | Response |
|---|---|---|
| ACCORDING TO THE TITLE OF MEL'S 1995 FILM, THIS VAMPIRE IS "DEAD AND LOVING IT" | **$100** | WHO IS |
| IT'S TWUE! IT'S TWUE! MADELINE KAHN PLAYED SINGER LILI VON SHTUPP IN THIS UPROARIOUS WESTERN | **$200** | WHAT IS |
| IN THIS FILM ZERO MOSTEL SCHEMES TO SELL 25,000 PERCENT OF A PLAY HE'S PUTTING ON | **$300** | WHAT IS |
| TERI GARR PLAYED A SEXY BLONDE NAMED INGA & PETER BOYLE WAS A MONSTER IN THIS FILM | **$400** | WHAT IS |
| "HISTORY OF THE WORLD—PART I" FEATURED MEL AS MOSES, TORQUEMADA & THE WAITER AT THIS BIBLICAL DINNER | **$500** | WHAT IS |

# JEOPARDY!™

# MEL BROOKS MOVIES

| | | |
|---|---|---|
| **$100** | WHO IS DRACULA? | **$100** |
| **$200** | WHAT IS "BLAZING SADDLES"? | **$200** |
| **$300** | WHAT IS "THE PRODUCERS"? | **$300** |
| **$400** | WHAT IS "YOUNG FRANKENSTEIN"? | **$400** |
| **$500** | WHAT IS THE LAST SUPPER? | **$500** |

# JEOPARDY!

## ODD WORDS

| | | |
|---|---|---|
| PEOPLE WERE AURIFIED BY KING MIDAS, MEANING HE TURNED THEM INTO THIS | **$100** | WHAT IS |
| THIS INSECT STORES POLLEN IN A CORBICULA, A LITTLE BASKET ON ITS BODY | **$200** | WHAT IS |
| A WOUBIT IS A HAIRY ONE OF THESE, MOST OFTEN THE ONE THAT BECOMES A TIGER MOTH | **$300** | WHAT IS |
| TO CANTILLATE IS TO DO THIS (MAYBE TO AN OLD GREGORIAN ONE) | **$400** | WHAT IS |
| A MAIKO IS AN APPRENTICE ONE OF THESE WOMEN WHO ENTERTAIN MEN IN JAPAN | **$500** | WHAT IS |

# JEOPARDY!

## ODD WORDS

$100 — WHAT IS GOLD? — $100

$200 — WHAT IS A BEE? — $200

$300 — WHAT IS A CATERPILLAR? — $300

$400 — WHAT IS CHANT? — $400

$500 — WHAT IS A GEISHA? — $500

# JEOPARDY!

## NICKNAMES

| | | |
|---|---|---|
| IVAN I WAS IVAN MONEYBAG, IVAN II WAS IVAN THE RED & IVAN IV WAS THIS | **$100** | WHAT IS |
| THIS "LUCKY" MOBSTER'S LUCK RAN OUT AT THE NAPLES AIRPORT ON JANUARY 26, 1962 | **$200** | WHO IS |
| BUCK TAYLOR, A STAR OF BUFFALO BILL'S WILD WEST SHOW, EARNED THIS "ROYAL" NICK-NAME BEFORE ROY ROGERS | **$300** | WHAT IS |
| WE PRESUME THIS VIRGINIAN FELT GOOD ABOUT HIS NICKNAME, "THE ERA-OF-GOOD-FEELING PRESIDENT" | **$400** | WHO IS |
| SOME CALLED THIS "MESSIAH" COMPOSER "THE THUNDERBOLT" AFTER MOZART SAID HE STRUCK LIKE ONE | **$500** | WHO IS |

# JEOPARDY!

## NICKNAMES

**$100** — WHAT IS IVAN THE TERRIBLE? — **$100**

**$200** — WHO IS CHARLES "LUCKY" LUCIANO? (ACCEPT: LUCIANA) — **$200**

**$300** — WHAT IS "KING OF THE COWBOYS"? — **$300**

**$400** — WHO IS JAMES MONROE? — **$400**

**$500** — WHO IS GEORGE FREDERICK HANDEL? — **$500**

194

# DOUBLE JEOPARDY!

## HISTORY BOOKS

| Clue | Value | Response |
|------|-------|----------|
| THIS 1997 STEVEN SPIELBERG FILM RENEWED INTEREST IN WILLIAM OWEN'S HISTORY "BLACK MUTINY" | $200 | WHAT IS |
| SHELBY FOOTE'S 3-VOLUME CIVIL WAR HISTORY ENDS WITH THE TOME "RED RIVER TO" THIS SURRENDER SITE | $400 | WHAT IS |
| STEPHEN AMBROSE'S "UNDAUNTED COURAGE" EXPLORES THE FRIENDSHIP OF MERIWETHER LEWIS & THIS PRESIDENT | $600 | WHO IS |
| BARBARA TUCHMAN WON HER FIRST PULITZER FOR THIS HISTORY OF THE BEGINNING OF WORLD WAR I | $800 | WHAT IS |
| THE AUTHOR OF "THE GALLIC WAR" WROTE IN THE THIRD PERSON, REFERRING TO HIMSELF BY THIS ONE-WORD TITLE | $1000 | WHAT IS |

# DOUBLE JEOPARDY!

## HISTORY BOOKS

| | | |
|---|---|---|
| **$200** | WHAT IS "AMISTAD"? | **$200** |
| **$400** | WHAT IS APPOMATTOX? | **$400** |
| **$600** | WHO IS THOMAS JEFFERSON? | **$600** |
| **$800** | WHAT IS "THE GUNS OF AUGUST"? | **$800** |
| **$1000** | WHAT IS CAESAR? | **$1000** |

# DOUBLE JEOPARDY!

## PHONY EXPRESS

| Clue | Value | Response |
|------|-------|----------|
| THE "CON" IN "CON MAN" IS SHORT FOR THIS | **$200** | WHAT IS |
| PYRITE GOT THIS NAME WHEN MANY PROSPECTORS MISTOOK IT FOR A MORE VALUABLE MINERAL | **$400** | WHAT IS |
| POSING AS ARABS WITH LOTS OF CASH, THE FBI CAUGHT 7 MEMBERS OF CONGRESS IN THIS 1970s STING OPERATION | **$600** | WHAT IS |
| HE SERVED TIME FOR FRAUD AFTER WRITING A FAKE HOWARD HUGHES BIOGRAPHY | **$800** | WHO IS |
| DUMMKOPFS! THIS GERMAN NEWS-MAGAZINE PAID MILLIONS FOR FORGED DIARIES OF ADOLF HITLER IN 1983 | **$1000** | WHAT IS |

# DOUBLE JEOPARDY!

## PHONY EXPRESS

| $200 | WHAT IS CONFIDENCE? | $200 |
| $400 | WHAT IS FOOL'S GOLD? | $400 |
| $600 | WHAT IS ABSCAM? (ACCEPT: ARAB SCAM) | $600 |
| $800 | WHO IS CLIFFORD IRVING? | $800 |
| $1000 | WHAT IS STERN MAGAZINE? | $1000 |

# DOUBLE JEOPARDY!

## BRIT ROCK

| | | |
|---|---|---|
| MICK JAGGER FIRST MET THIS FUTURE BANDMATE IN PRIMARY SCHOOL WHEN THEY WERE 7 | **$200** | WHO IS |
| IN 1984 THEY HAD A HIT WITH THE BOUNCY "WAKE ME UP BEFORE YOU GO-GO" | **$400** | WHAT IS |
| THIS "DARK" HEAVY METAL BAND OF THE 1970S CONSISTED OF BILL WARD, TONY IOMMI, GEEZER BUTLER & OZZY OSBOURNE | **$600** | WHAT IS |
| THIS BAND BEST KNOWN FOR THEIR 1985 HIT "WALKING ON SUNSHINE" WON THE 1997 EUROVISION SONG CONTEST | **$800** | WHAT IS |
| THIS OFTEN-GLOOMY GROUP HAS LONG BEEN LED BY LIPSTICK-SPORTING ROBERT SMITH | **$1000** | WHAT IS |

# DOUBLE JEOPARDY!

## BRIT ROCK

$200 — WHO IS KEITH RICHARDS? (ACCEPT: KEITH RICHARD) — $200

$400 — WHAT IS WHAM! (UK)? — $400

$600 — WHAT IS BLACK SABBATH? — $600

$800 — WHAT IS KATRINA & THE WAVES? — $800

$1000 — WHAT IS THE CURE? — $1000

# DOUBLE JEOPARDY!

## TOUGH SHAKESPEARE

| | | |
|---|---|---|
| SHYLOCK IS OUTWITTED IN COURT IN ACT IV OF THIS PLAY | **$200** | WHAT IS |
| THIS "TEMPEST" MAGIC-MAKER HAS A DAUGHTER NAMED MIRANDA & A SPRITELY SERVANT NAMED ARIEL | **$400** | WHO IS |
| PERSON TO WHOM HAMLET ADDRESSES HIS DYING WORDS | **$600** | WHO IS |
| ACT III OF THIS PLAY OPENS INSIDE KING PRIAM'S PALACE IN TROY | **$800** | WHAT IS |
| MISTRESS FORD & MISTRESS PAGE ARE THE SAUCY SPOUSES WHO TRICK & TORMENT FALSTAFF IN THIS COMEDY | **$1000** | WHAT IS |

# DOUBLE JEOPARDY!

## TOUGH SHAKESPEARE

| | | |
|---|---|---|
| **$200** | WHAT IS "THE MERCHANT OF VENICE"? | **$200** |
| **$400** | WHO IS PROSPERO? | **$400** |
| **$600** | WHO IS HORATIO? | **$600** |
| **$800** | WHAT IS "TROILUS AND CRESSIDA"? | **$800** |
| **$1000** | WHAT IS "THE MERRY WIVES OF WINDSOR"? | **$1000** |

# DOUBLE JEOPARDY!

## IMPORTS

| | | |
|---|---|---|
| ON APRIL 14, 1927 THIS COMPANY'S FIRST CAR CAME OFF ITS GOTHENBURG, SWEDEN ASSEMBLY LINE | $200 | WHAT IS |
| THIS BRAND OF WATER COMES FROM A NATURAL SPRING IN VERGEZE | $400 | WHAT IS |
| IN 1900 THIS JAPANESE COMPANY BEGAN PRODUCTION OF ITS UPRIGHT PIANOS; IN 1954, ITS MOTORCYCLES | $600 | WHAT IS |
| FOR 177 YEARS, UNTIL 1936, GUINNESS BREWED ALL OF ITS STOUT IN THIS CITY | $800 | WHAT IS |
| GIULIANA & LUCIANO'S UNITED COLORS COMPANY | $1000 | WHAT IS |

# DOUBLE JEOPARDY!

## IMPORTS

**$200**   WHAT IS VOLVO?   **$200**

**$400**   WHAT IS PERRIER?
(ACCEPT: VITTEL)   **$400**

**$600**   WHAT IS YAMAHA?   **$600**

**$800**   WHAT IS DUBLIN?   **$800**

**$1000**   WHAT IS BENETTON?   **$1000**

# DOUBLE JEOPARDY!

## TOM SWIFTIES

| | | |
|---|---|---|
| IT'S THE SATIRICAL WAY TOM SAID, "I LIKE TO PRESS MY OWN CLOTHES" | **$200** | WHAT IS |
| IT'S THE SECRET OR ENIGMATIC WAY TOM SAID, "LET'S GO LOOK AT THOSE TOMBS" | **$400** | WHAT IS |
| "I SENT A FOOD PACKAGE OVERSEAS", SAID TOM THIS WAY; IT'S ALSO HOW PORCUPINES MAKE LOVE | **$600** | WHAT IS |
| TOM TALKS ABOUT GLOVES INTERMITTENTLY; THE WAY HE TALKS ABOUT MAGAZINES IS THIS SYNONYM | **$800** | WHAT IS |
| IF YOU THINK DOGGEDLY ABOUT HIS HOARSE VOICE, YOU'LL KNOW IT'S HOW TOM SAID "MUSH!" | **$1000** | WHAT IS |

# DOUBLE JEOPARDY!

## TOM SWIFTIES

| | | |
|---|---|---|
| **$200** | WHAT IS IRONICALLY? | **$200** |
| **$400** | WHAT IS CRYPTICALLY? | **$400** |
| **$600** | WHAT IS CAREFULLY? | **$600** |
| **$800** | WHAT IS PERIODICALLY? | **$800** |
| **$1000** | WHAT IS HUSKILY? | **$1000** |

# FINAL JEOPARDY!

## VOLCANOES

THE 5 HIGHEST VOLCANOES
ON EARTH ARE LOCATED IN
THESE MOUNTAINS

WHAT ARE

# FINAL JEOPARDY!

## VOLCANOES

WHAT ARE THE ANDES?

# JEOPARDY!

## COMING TO AMERICA

| | | |
|---|---|---|
| CHINESE IMMIGRANTS BEGAN TO ARRIVE IN CALIFORNIA JUST BEFORE THIS 1849 "RUSH" | **$100** | WHAT IS |
| IN 1634 CATHOLICS COULD FIND REFUGE IN THIS COLONY FOUNDED BY CECIL CALVERT, LORD BALTIMORE | **$200** | WHAT IS |
| EUROPEANS WHO CAME TO AMERICA AS THIS KIND OF "SERVANT" PROMISED TO WORK FOR YEARS TO PAY THEIR PASSAGE | **$300** | WHAT IS |
| PEOPLE WHO EMIGRATE TO AMERICA FROM THIS COUNTRY ARE KNOWN AS ISSEI BACK HOME | **$400** | WHAT IS |
| FEW OF THE PENNSYLVANIA DUTCH CAME FROM HOLLAND; MOST CAME FROM THIS PRESENT-DAY COUNTRY | **$500** | WHAT IS |

# JEOPARDY!

## COMING TO AMERICA

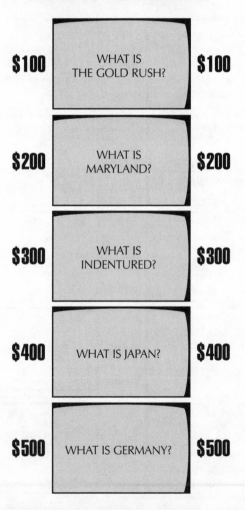

$100 — WHAT IS THE GOLD RUSH? — $100

$200 — WHAT IS MARYLAND? — $200

$300 — WHAT IS INDENTURED? — $300

$400 — WHAT IS JAPAN? — $400

$500 — WHAT IS GERMANY? — $500

# JEOPARDY!™

## POWERFUL WOMEN

| | | |
|---|---|---|
| THE FALKLAND ISLANDS WAR TESTED THE METTLE OF THIS "IRON LADY" | **$100** | WHO IS |
| BILL CLINTON MADE THIS TOUGH-TALKING MIAMIAN THE NATION'S NO. 1 COP | **$200** | WHO IS |
| IN 1988, 9 YEARS AFTER HER FATHER'S EXECUTION, SHE BECAME PRIME MINISTER OF PAKISTAN | **$300** | WHO IS |
| SHE WAS PUBLISHER OF THE WASHINGTON POST DURING WATERGATE | **$400** | WHO IS |
| THIS NFL TEAM OWNER MOVED HER RAMS FROM CALIFORNIA TO MISSOURI | **$500** | WHO IS |

# JEOPARDY!

## POWERFUL WOMEN

$100 — WHO IS MARGARET THATCHER? — $100

$200 — WHO IS JANET RENO? — $200

$300 — WHO IS BENAZIR BHUTTO? — $300

$400 — WHO IS KATHERINE GRAHAM? — $400

$500 — WHO IS GEORGIA (ROSENBLOOM) FRONTIERE? — $500

# JEOPARDY!

## PUDDING

| Clue | Value | Response |
|------|-------|----------|
| IT'S TRADITIONAL TO SERVE PLUM PUDDING ON THIS HOLIDAY, BUT DON'T PUT ANY PLUMS IN IT | **$100** | WHAT IS |
| IN "THROUGH THE LOOKING-GLASS", THE PUDDING REPRIMANDS THIS GIRL FOR CUTTING A SLICE OF HIM | **$200** | WHO IS |
| OF SPOTTED DICK, SPOTTED DARWIN OR SPOTTED DUDLEY, THE ONE THAT REALLY IS AN ENGLISH PUDDING | **$300** | WHAT IS |
| IN THE 1960s THIS BRAND THRILLED KIDS BY ADDING PINEAPPLE CREAM TO ITS LINE OF INSTANT PUDDINGS | **$400** | WHAT IS |
| LUCKILY, THIS "PUD-DING" SERVED WITH ROAST BEEF DOESN'T CONTAIN THE TERRIERS OF THE SAME NAME | **$500** | WHAT IS |

# JEOPARDY!™

## PUDDING

| | | |
|---|---|---|
| **$100** | WHAT IS CHRISTMAS? | **$100** |
| **$200** | WHO IS ALICE? | **$200** |
| **$300** | WHAT IS SPOTTED DICK? | **$300** |
| **$400** | WHAT IS JELL-O? | **$400** |
| **$500** | WHAT IS YORKSHIRE PUDDING? | **$500** |

# JEOPARDY!

## POP STARS

| | | |
|---|---|---|
| IN ADDITION TO HIS OWN BANDS, THIS GUITARIST HAS PLAYED WITH THE YARDBIRDS, CREAM & DEREK & THE DOMINOS | **$100** | WHO IS |
| B.B. KING MADE A GUEST APPEARANCE ON THIS GROUP'S "RATTLE AND HUM" ALBUM | **$200** | WHO ARE |
| "I HEARD IT THROUGH THE GRAPEVINE" THAT HE WAS ONCE A SESSION DRUMMER FOR SMOKEY ROBINSON | **$300** | WHO IS |
| NIRVANA DRUMMER DAVE GROHL WENT ON TO FORM THIS "COMBATIVE" BAND | **$400** | WHO ARE |
| JIM SEALS & THIS PARTNER TOURED WITH THE CHAMPS IN 1958, BUT DIDN'T HAVE A HIT AS A DUO UNTIL 1972 | **$500** | WHO IS |

# JEOPARDY!

## POP STARS

| | | |
|---|---|---|
| **$100** | WHO IS ERIC CLAPTON? | **$100** |
| **$200** | WHO ARE U2? | **$200** |
| **$300** | WHO IS MARVIN GAYE? | **$300** |
| **$400** | WHO ARE THE FOO FIGHTERS? | **$400** |
| **$500** | WHO IS DASH CROFTS? | **$500** |

# JEOPARDY!

## '90s FICTION

| Clue | Value | Response |
|------|-------|----------|
| IN 1997 IRA LEVIN DELIVERED "SON OF ROSEMARY", THE SEQUEL TO THIS NOVEL | $100 | WHAT IS |
| "THIS KIND OF CERTAINTY COMES ONLY ONCE", ROBERT TELLS FRANCESCA IN THIS BESTSELLING LOVE STORY | $200 | WHAT IS |
| IN "THE FOURTH K", MARIO PUZO PUT A NEW MEMBER OF THIS POLITICAL FAMILY IN THE WHITE HOUSE | $300 | WHO ARE |
| THIS 1993 JAMES REDFIELD BOOK HAS BEEN DESCRIBED AS "AN ADVENTURE IN PURSUIT OF A SPIRITUAL MYSTERY" | $400 | WHAT IS |
| THIS "BELOVED" AUTHOR SET HER NOVEL "PARADISE" IN THE FICTIONAL ALL-BLACK TOWN OF RUBY, OKLAHOMA | $500 | WHO IS |

# JEOPARDY!

## '90s FICTION

| | | |
|---|---|---|
| **$100** | WHAT IS "ROSEMARY'S BABY"? | **$100** |
| **$200** | WHAT IS "THE BRIDGES OF MADISON COUNTY"? | **$200** |
| **$300** | WHO ARE THE KENNEDYS? | **$300** |
| **$400** | WHAT IS "THE CELESTINE PROPHECY'? | **$400** |
| **$500** | WHO IS TONI MORRISON? | **$500** |

# JEOPARDY!

## WE THE "PEOPLE"

| | | |
|---|---|---|
| ACCORDING TO LYRICIST BOB MERRILL, "PEOPLE WHO NEED PEOPLE ARE" THIS | **$100** | WHAT IS |
| IN 1997 BILL COSBY WON FAVORITE MALE IN A NEW SERIES, HIS 15th OF THESE AWARDS | **$200** | WHAT ARE |
| THIS PHRASE FOR THE JEWS REFERS TO EXODUS 19:6, "YE SHALL BE UNTO ME . . . A HOLY NATION" | **$300** | WHAT IS |
| YOU CAN TOUR SCENIC DOWNTOWN DETROIT OR MIAMI ON THIS TYPE OF MASS TRANSIT SYSTEM | **$400** | WHAT IS |
| FOUNDED IN 1965, THIS "ELEVATING" ORGANIZA-TION LETS STUDENTS COMBINE INTER-NATIONAL TRAVEL & MUSICAL PERFORMANCE | **$500** | WHAT IS |

# JEOPARDY!

## WE THE "PEOPLE"

**$100** — WHAT IS "THE LUCKIEST PEOPLE IN THE WORLD"? — **$100**

**$200** — WHAT ARE THE PEOPLE'S CHOICE AWARDS? — **$200**

**$300** — WHAT IS THE CHOSEN PEOPLE? — **$300**

**$400** — WHAT IS A PEOPLE MOVER? — **$400**

**$500** — WHAT IS UP WITH PEOPLE? — **$500**

# DOUBLE JEOPARDY!

## ARTISTS

| | | |
|---|---|---|
| IN THE 1870s, BEFORE HE MOVED TO TAHITI, HE WAS STRONGLY INFLUENCED BY CAMILLE PISSARRO | **$200** | WHO IS |
| YOU CAN SEE HIS UNFINISHED "RONDANINI PIETA" AT THE CASTELLO SFORZESCO IN MILAN | **$400** | WHO IS |
| A NEW MUSEUM DEVOTED TO THIS FLOWERS-&-SKULLS ARTIST OPENED IN SANTA FE IN 1997 | **$600** | WHO IS |
| IN 1888 HE PAINTED A "CAFE TERRACE AT NIGHT" AS WELL AS "THE NIGHT CAFE" | **$800** | WHO IS |
| PAINTER MARGARETT SARGENT, WHO LIVED UNTIL 1978, WAS A COUSIN OF THIS SOCIETY PORTRAITIST | **$1000** | WHO IS |

# DOUBLE JEOPARDY!

## ARTISTS

$200 — WHO IS PAUL GAUGUIN? — $200

$400 — WHO IS MICHELANGELO? — $400

$600 — WHO IS GEORGIA O'KEEFFE? — $600

$800 — WHO IS VINCENT VAN GOGH? — $800

$1000 — WHO IS JOHN SINGER SARGENT? — $1000

# DOUBLE JEOPARDY!

## STRIFE WITH FATHER

| | | |
|---|---|---|
| SHE WHACKED HER STEPMOM, SAW WHAT SHE'D DONE, THEN "GAVE HER FATHER 41" | **$200** | WHO IS |
| THANKS TO AN ANGEL, ABRAHAM DIDN'T MAKE HIM THE ULTIMATE SACRIFICE | **$400** | WHO IS |
| IT'S PRETTY "COMPLEX" HOW HE MANAGED TO KILL HIS FATHER, SOLVE THE SPHINX' RIDDLE & MARRY HIS MOTHER | **$600** | WHO IS |
| IN 1989 JOSE & KITTY PAID DEARLY BECAUSE THESE 2 ALLEGEDLY COULDN'T WAIT FOR THEIR BEVERLY HILLS INHERITANCE | **$800** | WHO ARE |
| EXECUTED IN UTAH IN 1977, HE TOLD HIS BROTHER THAT THEIR FATHER WAS THE FIRST PERSON HE EVER WANTED TO MURDER | **$1000** | WHO IS |

# DOUBLE JEOPARDY!

## STRIFE WITH FATHER

**$200**    WHO IS LIZZIE BORDEN?    **$200**

**$400**    WHO IS ISAAC?    **$400**

**$600**    WHO IS OEDIPUS?    **$600**

**$800**    WHO ARE LYLE & ERIK MENENDEZ?    **$800**

**$1000**    WHO IS GARY GILMORE?    **$1000**

# DOUBLE JEOPARDY!

## TOUGH TV

| | | |
|---|---|---|
| ARTE JOHNSON WAS THE ONLY PERFORMER TO WIN AN EMMY FOR HIS WORK ON THIS COMEDY-VARIETY SERIES | **$200** | WHAT IS |
| NANTUCKET MEMORIAL AIRPORT DOUBLED FOR THE FICTIONAL TOM NEVERS FIELD ON THIS SITCOM | **$400** | WHAT IS |
| THIS ACTION SHOW STARRING RICHARD DEAN ANDERSON IS A FAVORITE OF MARGE SIMPSON'S SISTERS | **$600** | WHAT IS |
| THIS "MARY TYLER MOORE SHOW" SPINOFF STARRED CLORIS LEACHMAN AS THE TITLE CHARACTER | **$800** | WHAT IS |
| MONICA EVANS & CAROLE SHELLEY PLAYED THE PIGEON SISTERS ON THIS SITCOM, AS WELL AS IN THE STAGE & FILM VERSIONS | **$1000** | WHAT IS |

# DOUBLE JEOPARDY!

## TOUGH TV

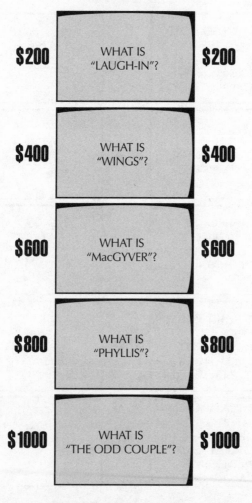

$200    WHAT IS "LAUGH-IN"?    $200

$400    WHAT IS "WINGS"?    $400

$600    WHAT IS "MacGYVER"?    $600

$800    WHAT IS "PHYLLIS"?    $800

$1000    WHAT IS "THE ODD COUPLE"?    $1000

# DOUBLE JEOPARDY!

## LATIN LESSON

| | | |
|---|---|---|
| "ANNUS MIRABILIS" IS A REMARKABLE ONE OF THESE | **$200** | WHAT IS |
| ANTE BELLUM MEANS "BEFORE" THIS, SOMETHING MANY PEOPLE ARE ANTI- | **$400** | WHAT IS |
| IN "JULIUS CAESAR" SHAKESPEARE TAUGHT US THIS PHRASE MEANING "YOU ALSO" | **$600** | WHAT IS |
| BRITISH RULERS HAVE THE TITLE FIDEI DEFENSOR, MEANING THIS | **$800** | WHAT IS |
| THIS 2-WORD PHRASE REFERS TO THE PROOF A CRIME HAS BEEN COMMITTED, NOT NECESSARILY THE MURDER VICTIM | **$1000** | WHAT IS |

# DOUBLE JEOPARDY!

## LATIN LESSON

| | |
|---|---|
| **$200** | WHAT IS A YEAR? | **$200** |
| **$400** | WHAT IS WAR? | **$400** |
| **$600** | WHAT IS ET TU? | **$600** |
| **$800** | WHAT IS DEFENDER OF THE FAITH? | **$800** |
| **$1000** | WHAT IS CORPUS DELICTI? | **$1000** |

# DOUBLE JEOPARDY!

## ODD WEIGHTS & MEASURES

| | | |
|---|---|---|
| AN EXPLOSION RATED A MEGATON IS EQUAL TO THIS MANY TONS OF TNT | **$200** | WHAT IS |
| A UNIT OF CLOTH MEASURE EQUAL TO 2 1/4 INCHES, OR A CARPENTER'S ITEM WHOSE SIZE IS MEASURED IN PENNIES | **$400** | WHAT IS |
| IN SPAIN A BRAZA WAS EQUAL TO THE REACH OF THESE OUTSTRETCHED | **$600** | WHAT ARE |
| YOU'RE MAKING QUITE A "PIG" OF YOURSELF CONSUMING THIS MEASURE OF LIQUID EQUAL TO 63 GALLONS | **$800** | WHAT IS |
| A JUDITH KRANTZ TITLE WHICH ALSO COULD BE UNITS OF APOTHECARY WEIGHT, EQUAL TO 20 GRAINS EACH | **$1000** | WHAT IS |

# DOUBLE JEOPARDY!

## ODD WEIGHTS & MEASURES

| | | |
|---|---|---|
| **$200** | WHAT IS ONE MILLION? | **$200** |
| **$400** | WHAT IS A NAIL? | **$400** |
| **$600** | WHAT ARE THE ARMS? | **$600** |
| **$800** | WHAT IS A HOGSHEAD? | **$800** |
| **$1000** | WHAT IS "SCRUPLES"? | **$1000** |

# DOUBLE JEOPARDY!

## A RIVER RUNS THROUGH IT

| Clue | Value | Response |
|------|-------|----------|
| AT LONDON BRIDGE THIS RIVER IS ABOUT 800 FEET WIDE; AT ITS MOUTH, MORE THAN 5 MILES | $200 | WHAT IS |
| IT'S THE ONLY MAJOR AFRICAN RIVER EMPTYING INTO THE MEDITERRANEAN SEA | $400 | WHAT IS |
| THE PLATTE RIVER JOINS THE MISSOURI NEAR PLATTSMOUTH IN THIS STATE | $600 | WHAT IS |
| ABOUT 60% OF THIS "MOTHER" RIVER OF RUSSIA'S WATER FLOW IS FROM SNOW; THE REST IS FROM GROUNDWATER & RAIN | $800 | WHAT IS |
| COLUMBUS FIRST SIGHTED THIS VENEZUELAN RIVER IN 1498, BUT IT WASN'T EXPLORED UNTIL 33 YEARS LATER | $1000 | WHAT IS |

# DOUBLE JEOPARDY!

## A RIVER RUNS THROUGH IT

$200    WHAT IS THE THAMES RIVER?    $200

$400    WHAT IS THE NILE RIVER?    $400

$600    WHAT IS NEBRASKA?    $600

$800    WHAT IS THE VOLGA RIVER?    $800

$1000    WHAT IS THE ORINOCO RIVER?    $1000

# FINAL JEOPARDY!

## COMPOSERS

WHEN "FANTASIA" WAS
RELEASED IN 1940, HE WAS
THE ONLY ONE OF ITS
COMPOSERS STILL ALIVE
TO HEAR HIS MUSIC

WHO IS

# FINAL JEOPARDY!

## COMPOSERS

WHO IS
IGOR (FYODOROVICH)
STRAVINSKY?

# JEOPARDY!

## READ AMERICAN!

| | | |
|---|---|---|
| "THE CASK OF AMONTILLADO" IS AMONG HIS MACABRE MASTERPIECES | **$100** | WHO IS |
| MARK TWAIN'S TALE OF SWITCHED IDENTITIES IN TUDOR ENGLAND | **$200** | WHAT IS |
| STARTING IN 1914, HE WROTE 26 TARZAN BOOKS | **$300** | WHO IS |
| JAMES FENIMORE COOPER WROTE 5 OF THESE "TALES" NAMED FOR AN ALIAS OF NATTY BUMPPO | **$400** | WHAT ARE |
| HE COMBINED FANTASY & SATIRE IN WORKS LIKE "CAT'S CRADLE" & "GOD BLESS YOU, MR. ROSEWATER" | **$500** | WHO IS |

# JEOPARDY!

## READ AMERICAN!

**$100** | WHO IS EDGAR ALLAN POE? | **$100**

**$200** | WHAT IS "THE PRINCE AND THE PAUPER"? | **$200**

**$300** | WHO IS EDGAR RICE BURROUGHS? | **$300**

**$400** | WHAT ARE LEATHERSTOCKING TALES? | **$400**

**$500** | WHO IS KURT VONNEGUT (JR.)? | **$500**

# JEOPARDY!

## OLD YORK

| Clue | Value | Response |
|---|---|---|
| IN 1990 YORK REINSTATED THIS AGE-OLD JOB OF CALLING THE LOCAL NEWS THROUGH THE CITY | **$100** | WHAT IS |
| YOU CAN'T MISS YORK MINSTER, ENGLAND'S LARGEST CHURCH IN THIS STYLE NAMED FOR A GERMANIC TRIBE | **$200** | WHAT IS |
| YORK IS A HUB OF THIS TYPE OF TRANSPORTATION & HAS A NATIONAL MUSEUM DEDICATED TO IT | **$300** | WHAT IS |
| ALAS, POOR YORK! IT WAS BURNED BY THIS NEW RULER OF ENGLAND IN THE 11th CENTURY | **$400** | WHO IS |
| THESE MEDIEVAL PLAYS, NONE BY AGATHA CHRISTIE, ARE PERFORMED IN A CYCLE AT YORK EVERY 4 YEARS | **$500** | WHAT ARE |

# JEOPARDY!™

## OLD YORK

| | | |
|---|---|---|
| **$100** | WHAT IS THE TOWN CRIER? | **$100** |
| **$200** | WHAT IS GOTHIC? | **$200** |
| **$300** | WHAT IS THE RAILROAD? | **$300** |
| **$400** | WHO IS WILLIAM THE CONQUEROR? (ACCEPT: WILLIAM I) | **$400** |
| **$500** | WHAT ARE MYSTERY PLAYS? | **$500** |

# JEOPARDY!

## HELLO, DALAI

| | | |
|---|---|---|
| ACCORDING TO THE DALAI LAMA'S WEB SITE, "DALAI" MEANS THIS, PRESUMABLY THE PACIFIC ONE | **$100** | WHAT IS |
| THE DALAI LAMA'S MOST FAMOUS DISCIPLE, THIS ACTOR PUBLISHED A BOOK OF PHOTOS OF BUDDHIST CULTURE | **$200** | WHO IS |
| THE DALAI LAMA IS THE SPIRITUAL REINCARNATION OF THIS ENLIGHTENED ONE, FORMERLY KNOWN AS GAUTAMA | **$300** | WHO IS |
| AFTER HIS EXILE IN 1959, THE DALAI LAMA WENT TO LIVE IN THE HIMALAYAN TOWN OF DHARMSALA IN THIS COUNTRY | **$400** | WHAT IS |
| AMONG BOOKS THE DALAI LAMA PUBLISHED IS "THE ART OF" THIS: "A HANDBOOK FOR LIVING" | **$500** | WHAT IS |

# JEOPARDY!

## HELLO, DALAI

| | | |
|---|---|---|
| **$100** | WHAT IS OCEAN? | **$100** |
| **$200** | WHO IS RICHARD GERE? | **$200** |
| **$300** | WHO IS BUDDHA? | **$300** |
| **$400** | WHAT IS INDIA? | **$400** |
| **$500** | WHAT IS HAPPINESS? | **$500** |

# JEOPARDY!

## FAMILIAR PHRASES

| | | |
|---|---|---|
| IT'S "THE SHORTEST DISTANCE BETWEEN TWO POINTS" | **$100** | WHAT IS |
| IT'S WHERE SOMETHING EMBARRASSING IS SWEPT | **$200** | WHAT IS |
| POOL TABLE PIECE YOU DON'T WANT TO BE "BEHIND" | **$300** | WHAT IS |
| SHIFTING YOUR DEBTS IS "ROBBING PETER TO PAY" THIS SAINT | **$400** | WHO IS |
| ALEXANDER POPE CRITICIZED THOSE WHO CLAIMED TO BE AUTHORITIES WITH "FOOLS RUSH IN WHERE ANGELS" DO THIS | **$500** | WHAT IS |

# JEOPARDY!™

## FAMILIAR PHRASES

| | | |
|---|---|---|
| **$100** | WHAT IS A STRAIGHT LINE? | **$100** |
| **$200** | WHAT IS UNDER THE RUG? (ACCEPT: UNDER THE CARPET) | **$200** |
| **$300** | WHAT IS THE EIGHT BALL? | **$300** |
| **$400** | WHO IS PAUL? | **$400** |
| **$500** | WHAT IS "FEAR TO TREAD"? | **$500** |

# JEOPARDY!

## CAPTAINS COURAGEOUS

| | | |
|---|---|---|
| IN AN EARLY ACCOUNT OF JAMESTOWN'S FIRST YEAR, HE MADE NO MENTION OF HIS RESCUE BY POCAHONTAS | **$100** | WHO IS |
| A CITY & ISLAND IN BRITISH COLUMBIA ARE NAMED FOR THIS SEA CAPTAIN WHO EXPLORED THE AREA IN 1792 | **$200** | WHO IS |
| KING LOUIS XVI GAVE THIS AMERICAN REVOLUTIONARY FIGURE A GOLD SWORD & MADE HIM A CHEVALIER OF FRANCE | **$300** | WHO IS |
| IT TOOK HIM & HIS CREW 37 DAYS TO TRAVERSE THE SOUTH AMERICAN STRAIT NOW NAMED FOR HIM | **$400** | WHO IS |
| IN 1642 & 1643 THIS DUTCH CAPTAIN CIRCUMNAVIGATED AUSTRALIA WITHOUT SEEING IT | **$500** | WHO IS |

# JEOPARDY!

# CAPTAINS COURAGEOUS

$100 — WHO IS JOHN SMITH? — $100

$200 — WHO IS GEORGE VANCOUVER? — $200

$300 — WHO IS JOHN PAUL JONES? — $300

$400 — WHO IS FERDINAND MAGELLAN? — $400

$500 — WHO IS ABEL TASMAN? — $500

# JEOPARDY!™

# THE IMMORTAL ABBA

| | | |
|---|---|---|
| BILLBOARD CALLS THIS ABBA MORSE CODE PLEA THE "ONLY CHART HIT WHERE BOTH TITLE AND ARTIST ARE PALINDROMES" | $100 | WHAT IS |
| THIS TITLE TEEN BROUGHT ABBA THEIR FIRST U.S. NO. 1 HIT | $200 | WHO IS |
| 1978 TITLE IN WHICH ABBA ASKED YOU TO BE A BIT OF A GAMBLER | $300 | WHAT IS |
| THE 1994 FILM ABOUT THIS VEHICLE, "QUEEN OF THE DESERT", FEATURED THE MUSIC OF ABBA | $400 | WHAT IS |
| AGNETHA & ANNI-FRID ARE THE A'S IN THE GROUP'S NAME; BENNY & HIM ARE THE B'S | $500 | WHO IS |

# JEOPARDY!

## THE IMMORTAL ABBA

**$100** WHAT IS "SOS"? **$100**

**$200** WHO IS "DANCING QUEEN"? **$200**

**$300** WHAT IS "TAKE A CHANCE ON ME"? **$300**

**$400** WHAT IS PRISCILLA? **$400**

**$500** WHO IS BJORN (ULVAEUS)? **$500**

# DOUBLE JEOPARDY!

## SYMPHONIES

| | | |
|---|---|---|
| THE "PATHETIC" SYMPHONY IS BY THIS RUSSIAN WHO ALSO GAVE US THE CELEBRATORY "1812 OVERTURE" | $200 | WHO IS |
| COMPOSER CARL STALLING USED GRIEG'S "MARCH OF THE DWARFS" IN THE FIRST OF THESE DISNEY "SYMPHONIES" | $400 | WHAT ARE |
| MAHLER'S MASSIVE 8th IS THE "SYMPHONY OF" THIS MANY MUSICIANS, EQUAL TO 250 QUARTETS | $600 | WHAT IS |
| HAYDN'S 94th SYMPHONY IS CALLED THIS, LIKE A STARTLING TYPE OF PARTY | $800 | WHAT IS |
| ONE OF THE MOVEMENTS OF HOLST'S "THE PLANETS", OR THE NICKNAME OF MOZART'S SYMPHONY NO. 41 | $1000 | WHAT IS |

# DOUBLE JEOPARDY!

## SYMPHONIES

$200 — WHO IS PETER ILYICH TCHAIKOVSKY? — $200

$400 — WHAT ARE SILLY SYMPHONIES? — $400

$600 — WHAT IS 1,000? — $600

$800 — WHAT IS SURPRISE? — $800

$1000 — WHAT IS JUPITER? — $1000

# DOUBLE JEOPARDY!

## 1948

| Clue | Value | Response |
|---|---|---|
| DENMARK, NORWAY & SWEDEN COMBINED THEIR MAJOR AIRLINE COMPANIES INTO THIS ONE | **$200** | WHAT IS |
| ON THE THIRD BALLOT ON JUNE 24, THE REPUBLICAN NOMINATION FOR PRESIDENT WENT TO THIS GOVERNOR | **$400** | WHO IS |
| HE CAME INTO THE WORLD AT BUCKINGHAM PALACE ON NOVEMBER 14 | **$600** | WHO IS |
| A YOUNG MAN NAMED NORMAN MAILER GAINED FAME WITH THIS WAR NOVEL | **$800** | WHAT IS |
| TO LIFE, TO LIFE, TO THIS MAN, ELECTED PROVISIONAL PRESIDENT OF ISRAEL MAY 16, 1948 | **$1000** | WHO IS |

# DOUBLE JEOPARDY!

## 1948

$200 — WHAT IS SAS? (ACCEPT: SCANDINAVIAN AIRLINES SYSTEM) — $200

$400 — WHO IS THOMAS E. DEWEY? — $400

$600 — WHO IS PRINCE CHARLES? — $600

$800 — WHAT IS "THE NAKED AND THE DEAD"? — $800

$1000 — WHO IS CHAIM WEIZMANN? — $1000

# DOUBLE JEOPARDY!

## HOBBIES

| Clue | Value | Response |
|------|-------|----------|
| SOME PEOPLE RAISE BABY FOXES, CALLED THESE; SOME BUILD MODEL CARS FROM SETS OF PARTS, ALSO CALLED THESE | **$200** | WHAT ARE |
| TYPE OF HOBBYIST WHO KEEPS A "LIFE LIST" THAT MAY INCLUDE VIREOS & TANAGERS | **$400** | WHAT IS |
| IF YOU HAVEN'T TRIED THIS HOBBY WHOSE NAME INCLUDES "WORKING", YOU MAY BE A LATHE BLOOMER | **$600** | WHAT IS |
| THIS TYPE OF FISHING REQUIRES A "TIP-UP" DEVICE TO SIGNAL A BITE; MITTENS ARE ALSO USEFUL | **$800** | WHAT IS |
| IN THIS DEXTROUS HOBBY, A "CASCADE" MOVES BALLS OR PLATES IN A FIGURE 8; A "SHOWER" MOVES THEM IN A CIRCLE | **$1000** | WHAT IS |

# DOUBLE JEOPARDY!

## HOBBIES

| | |
|---|---|
| **$200** | WHAT ARE KITS? | **$200** |
| **$400** | WHAT IS A BIRDWATCHER? | **$400** |
| **$600** | WHAT IS WOODWORKING? (ACCEPT: METALWORKING) | **$600** |
| **$800** | WHAT IS ICE FISHING? | **$800** |
| **$1000** | WHAT IS JUGGLING? | **$1000** |

# DOUBLE JEOPARDY!

## SPORTS

| Clue | Value | Response |
|---|---|---|
| COMPETITION BEGAN IN 1900 FOR THIS CUP AWARDED TO A NATIONAL MEN'S TENNIS TEAM | **$200** | WHAT IS |
| ON SEPT. 23, 1926 THIS HEAVYWEIGHT BOXING CHAMP LOST HIS TITLE TO GENE TUNNEY IN A DECISION | **$400** | WHO IS |
| IN 1973 RON TURCOTTE RODE THIS HORSE TO THE FIRST TRIPLE CROWN VICTORY IN 25 YEARS | **$600** | WHAT IS |
| RED SOX SHORTSTOP & 1999 BATTING CHAMPION WHOSE FIRST NAME IS HIS FATHER'S, RAMON, SPELLED BACKWARDS | **$800** | WHO IS |
| THIS VIKINGS WIDE RECEIVER OUT OF MARSHALL HAD AN EXPLOSIVE ROOKIE YEAR IN 1998 | **$1000** | WHO IS |

# DOUBLE JEOPARDY!

## SPORTS

$200  WHAT IS THE DAVIS CUP?  $200

$400  WHO IS JACK DEMPSEY?  $400

$600  WHAT IS SECRETARIAT?  $600

$800  WHO IS NOMAR GARCIAPARRA?  $800

$1000  WHO IS RANDY MOSS?  $1000

# DOUBLE JEOPARDY!

## ITALIAN CITIES

| | | |
|---|---|---|
| A REGATTA HELD EACH SEPTEMBER IN THIS CITY FEATURES GONDOLA RACES ON THE GRAND CANAL | $200 | WHAT IS |
| SHAKESPEARE'S FEUDING MONTAGUES & CAPULETS WERE INSPIRED BY ACTUAL INCIDENTS IN THIS CITY | $400 | WHAT IS |
| THE WORLD'S MOST FAMOUS SHROUD WAS HOUSED IN THIS CITY STARTING IN 1578 | $600 | WHAT IS |
| THIS CITY'S PIAZZA DANTE CONTAINS THE HOUSE BELIEVED TO BE THAT OF CHRISTOPHER COLUMBUS | $800 | WHAT IS |
| CONDUCTOR ARTURO TOSCANINI WAS BORN IN THIS CITY FAMOUS FOR ITS CHEESE | $1000 | WHAT IS |

# DOUBLE JEOPARDY!

## ITALIAN CITIES

| $200 | WHAT IS VENICE? | $200 |
|---|---|---|
| $400 | WHAT IS VERONA? | $400 |
| $600 | WHAT IS TURIN? | $600 |
| $800 | WHAT IS GENOA? (ACCEPT: GENOVA) | $800 |
| $1000 | WHAT IS PARMA? | $1000 |

# DOUBLE JEOPARDY!

## WHO SAID THAT?

| | | |
|---|---|---|
| THE 1758 PREFACE TO HIS "POOR RICHARD'S ALMANAC" SAYS, "HE THAT LIVES UPON HOPE WILL DIE FASTING" | **$200** | WHO IS |
| THE NIGHT BEFORE HIS 1968 MURDER HE SAID, "I'M NOT WORRIED ABOUT ANYTHING. I'M NOT FEARING ANY MAN" | **$400** | WHO IS |
| COMEDIAN WHOSE MOST FAMOUS LINE WAS "TAKE MY WIFE— PLEASE!" | **$600** | WHO IS |
| "I CAN RESIST EVERY-THING EXCEPT TEMPTATION", HE WROTE IN "LADY WINDERMERE'S FAN" | **$800** | WHO IS |
| THIS FEMINIST SAID, "SOME OF US ARE BECOMING THE MEN WE WANTED TO MARRY" | **$1000** | WHO IS |

# DOUBLE JEOPARDY!™

## WHO SAID THAT?

| | | |
|---|---|---|
| $200 | WHO IS BENJAMIN FRANKLIN? | $200 |
| $400 | WHO IS MARTIN LUTHER KING JR.? | $400 |
| $600 | WHO IS HENNY YOUNGMAN? | $600 |
| $800 | WHO IS OSCAR WILDE? | $800 |
| $1000 | WHO IS GLORIA STEINEM? | $1000 |

# FINAL JEOPARDY!

## TELEVISION PERSONALITIES

HE WAS ORDAINED BY
PITTSBURGH PRESBYTERY IN
1962 WITH A CHARGE TO
WORK WITH CHILDREN
THROUGH THE MEDIA

WHO IS

# FINAL JEOPARDY!

## TELEVISION PERSONALITIES

WHO IS FRED ROGERS?
(ACCEPT: MISTER ROGERS)

# JEOPARDY!™

## THE LAND OF OZ

| | | |
|---|---|---|
| THIS PAVING MATERIAL OF THE ROAD TO THE EMERALD CITY IS IN NEED OF REPAIRS | **$100** | WHAT IS |
| THE "WIZARD" OF OZ IS FROM OMAHA, NEBRASKA, NOT FAR FROM THIS STATE WHERE DOROTHY LIVES | **$200** | WHAT IS |
| AS SEEN IN CHAPTER 2, THEY'RE ABOUT AS TALL AS DOROTHY & WEAR FOOT-HIGH POINTED HATS | **$300** | WHAT ARE |
| PART OF OZ IS POPULATED BY BREAKABLE PEOPLE MADE OF THIS, ALSO THE NAME OF A REAL COUNTRY | **$400** | WHAT IS |
| IN THE BOOK, THIS EVIL PERSONAGE HAS ONLY ONE EYE & HER SLAVES ARE CALLED WINKIES | **$500** | WHO IS |

261

# JEOPARDY!

## THE LAND OF OZ

**$100**  WHAT IS YELLOW BRICK?  **$100**

**$200**  WHAT IS KANSAS?  **$200**

**$300**  WHAT ARE MUNCHKINS?  **$300**

**$400**  WHAT IS CHINA?  **$400**

**$500**  WHO IS THE WICKED WITCH OF THE WEST?  **$500**

# JEOPARDY!

## FORTS

| Clue | Value | Response |
|------|-------|----------|
| THIS KENTUCKY FORT INCLUDES THE PATTON MUSEUM OF CAVALRY & ARMOR IN ADDITION TO ALL THAT GOLD | $100 | WHAT IS |
| THIS INDIANA CITY RECONSTRUCTED ITS NAMESAKE LOG STOCKADE IN THE 1970s | $200 | WHAT IS |
| FORT NECESSITY WAS BUILT BY THIS FUTURE GENERAL & IN 1754 WAS THE SITE OF HIS ONLY SURRENDER | $300 | WHO IS |
| HOME OF THE XVIII AIRBORNE CORPS, THIS N.C. FORT CAN BOAST IT WAS NAMED FOR A CONFEDERATE GENERAL | $400 | WHAT IS |
| THIS SEAT OF LARIMER COUNTY, COLORADO GREW UP AROUND A MILITARY OUTPOST BEGINNING IN THE 1860s | $500 | WHAT IS |

# JEOPARDY!

## FORTS

**$100** — WHAT IS FORT KNOX? — **$100**

**$200** — WHAT IS FORT WAYNE? — **$200**

**$300** — WHO IS GEORGE WASHINGTON? — **$300**

**$400** — WHAT IS FORT BRAGG? — **$400**

**$500** — WHAT IS FORT COLLINS? — **$500**

# JEOPARDY!

## 5 GUYS NAMED MOE

| | | |
|---|---|---|
| LAST NAME OF MOE OF THE THREE STOOGES | **$100** | WHAT IS |
| MOE STRAUSS FOUNDED THIS AUTO PARTS CHAIN ALONG WITH MANNY ROSENFIELD & JACK JACKSON | **$200** | WHAT IS |
| MAJOR LEAGUE CATCHER MOE BERG WAS ALSO A WWII SPY FOR THIS AGENCY, PRECURSOR OF THE CIA | **$300** | WHAT IS |
| TERM FOR THE TYPE OF COUNTRY MUSIC MOE BANDY PLAYS, THE CLUBS WHERE HE BEGAN, OR THE "QUEEN" HE SANG OF IN 1981 | **$400** | WHAT IS |
| THIS "KOOL" RAPPER'S ALBUM "HOW YA LIKE ME NOW" BEGAN A RIVALRY WITH LL COOL J | **$500** | WHO IS |

# JEOPARDY!

## 5 GUYS NAMED MOE

$100 — WHAT IS HOWARD? (ACCEPT: HOROWITZ) — $100

$200 — WHAT IS PEP BOYS? (ACCEPT: PEP AUTO SUPPLIES) — $200

$300 — WHAT IS THE OSS? (ACCEPT: OFFICE OF STRATEGIC SERVICES) — $300

$400 — WHAT IS HONKY TONK? — $400

$500 — WHO IS KOOL MOE DEE? — $500

# JEOPARDY!

## DRESS UP

| | | |
|---|---|---|
| DOGGONE! THESE CLASSIC SUEDE SHOES SHARE THEIR NAME WITH A SOUTHERN CORNMEAL TREAT | **$100** | WHAT ARE |
| "INVENTIVE" NAME FOR LEATHER SHOES & PURSES COATED WITH VARNISH FOR A HARD GLOSSY FINISH | **$200** | WHAT IS |
| IT'S A MONK'S HOOD OR A DRAPED NECKLINE FOR WOMEN THAT FALLS IN SOFT FOLDS | **$300** | WHAT IS |
| THIS FORM-FITTING BODYSUIT FOR DANCERS & ACROBATS IS NAMED FOR A 19th CENTURY FRENCH AERIALIST | **$400** | WHAT IS |
| IN MEXICO THIS LARGE BLACK VEIL IS COMMONLY WORN OVER A HIGH COMB | **$500** | WHAT IS |

# JEOPARDY!

## DRESS UP

| $100 | WHAT ARE HUSH PUPPIES? | $100 |
| $200 | WHAT IS PATENT (LEATHER)? | $200 |
| $300 | WHAT IS A COWL (NECK)? | $300 |
| $400 | WHAT IS A LEOTARD? | $400 |
| $500 | WHAT IS A MANTILLA? | $500 |

# JEOPARDY!

## THEIR SECRET IDENTITIES

| | | |
|---|---|---|
| DON DIEGO DE LA VEGA | **$100** | WHO IS |
| TV's DR. DAVID BANNER | **$200** | WHO IS |
| THE COMICS' PETER PARKER | **$300** | WHO IS |
| TV's BARBARA GORDON | **$400** | WHO IS |
| DUMAS' EDMOND DANTES | **$500** | WHO IS |

# JEOPARDY!

# THEIR SECRET IDENTITIES

| | |
|---|---|
| $100 | WHO IS ZORRO? | $100 |
| $200 | WHO IS THE (INCREDIBLE) HULK? | $200 |
| $300 | WHO IS SPIDER-MAN? | $300 |
| $400 | WHO IS BATGIRL? | $400 |
| $500 | WHO IS THE COUNT OF MONTE CRISTO? | $500 |

# JEOPARDY!

## "TEN"SION

| | | |
|---|---|---|
| SHE SHARED "MUSKRAT LOVE" WITH THE CAPTAIN | **$100** | WHO IS |
| INFLAMMATION NAMED FOR A SPORT & A JOINT | **$200** | WHAT IS |
| PSYCHIATRIST DICK DIVER IS A CENTRAL CHARACTER IN THIS JAZZ AGE NOVEL | **$300** | WHAT IS |
| NOTABLE NEPALESE NORGAY | **$400** | WHO IS |
| IF YOU WANT TO PEEK AT SPAIN'S HIGHEST PEAK, LOOK FOR EL TEIDE ON THIS ISLAND | **$500** | WHAT IS |

# JEOPARDY!

## "TEN"SION

**$100** — WHO IS (TONI) TENNILLE? — **$100**

**$200** — WHAT IS TENNIS ELBOW? — **$200**

**$300** — WHAT IS "TENDER IS THE NIGHT"? — **$300**

**$400** — WHO IS TENZING (NORGAY)? (ACCEPT: TENZIG) — **$400**

**$500** — WHAT IS TENERIFE? — **$500**

272

# DOUBLE JEOPARDY!

## THE LIBRARY OF ALEXANDRIA

| Clue | Value | Response |
|------|-------|----------|
| TO MAKE UP FOR DAMAGE JULIUS CAESAR DID TO THE LIBRARY, THIS MAN GAVE CLEOPATRA 200,000 MANUSCRIPTS | **$200** | WHO IS |
| LIBRARIAN ZENODOTUS DIVIDED THESE 2 HOMER WORKS INTO 24 BOOKS EACH | **$400** | WHAT IS |
| OFTEN SEEN AROUND THE STACKS WAS THIS "ELEMENTS" AUTHOR | **$600** | WHO IS |
| THIRD LIBRARIAN ERATOSTHENES DETERMINED THIS MEASUREMENT OF THE EARTH VERY CLOSE TO THE ACTUAL 25,000 MILES | **$800** | WHAT IS |
| THE FOURTH LIBRARIAN SHARED HIS NAME WITH THIS AUTHOR OF "THE BIRDS", WHOSE WORKS HE CRITIQUED | **$1000** | WHO IS |

# DOUBLE JEOPARDY!

## THE LIBRARY OF ALEXANDRIA

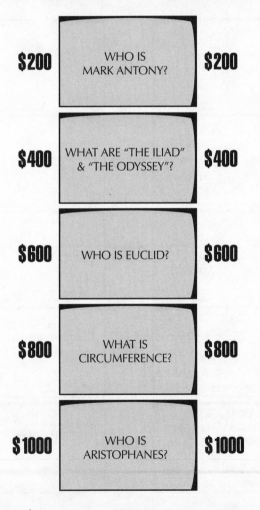

$200 — WHO IS MARK ANTONY? — $200

$400 — WHAT ARE "THE ILIAD" & "THE ODYSSEY"? — $400

$600 — WHO IS EUCLID? — $600

$800 — WHAT IS CIRCUMFERENCE? — $800

$1000 — WHO IS ARISTOPHANES? — $1000

# DOUBLE JEOPARDY!

## OPERATIC DEMISES

| | | |
|---|---|---|
| IN A BIBLICAL OPERA, THIS SHORN STRONGMAN REALLY BRINGS DOWN THE HOUSE | **$200** | WHO IS |
| A CRAP GAME ON CATFISH ROW TURNS DEADLY WHEN CROWN KILLS ROBBINS WITH A COTTON-HOOK IN THIS OPERA | **$400** | WHAT IS |
| IN A MELVILLE-INSPIRED OPERA, THIS YOUNG SAILOR IS HANGED FROM THE YARDARM OF THE H.M.S. INDOMITABLE | **$600** | WHO IS |
| IN "ELEGY FOR YOUNG LOVERS" 2 LOVERS EXPIRE WHILE SEARCHING FOR EDELWEISS IN THESE MOUNTAINS IN AUSTRIA | **$800** | WHAT ARE |
| IN A RICHARD STRAUSS OPERA, THIS DAUGHTER OF AGAMEMNON IS SO "COMPLEX" THAT SHE DANCES HERSELF TO DEATH | **$1000** | WHO IS |

# DOUBLE JEOPARDY!

## OPERATIC DEMISES

$200    WHO IS SAMSON?    $200

$400    WHAT IS "PORGY AND BESS"?    $400

$600    WHO IS BILLY BUDD?    $600

$800    WHAT ARE THE ALPS?    $800

$1000    WHO IS ELEKTRA?    $1000

# DOUBLE JEOPARDY!

## CELEBRATIONS

| Clue | Value | Response |
|------|-------|----------|
| NOVEMBER 3 IS THE NATIONAL DAY TO CELEBRATE THIS, BE IT TUNA FISH OR PEANUT BUTTER & JELLY | **$200** | WHAT IS |
| CONFEDERATE HEROES DAY IS CELEBRATED JANUARY 19, THE BIRTHDAY OF THIS GENERAL | **$400** | WHO IS |
| APPROPRIATELY, NATIONAL STRESS AWARENESS DAY IS OBSERVED ON THIS DATE, ONE DAY AFTER "TAX DAY" | **$600** | WHAT IS |
| DICTIONARY DAY, OCTOBER 16, CELEBRATES THE BIRTHDAY OF THIS AMERICAN LEXICOGRAPHER; LOOK IT UP! | **$800** | WHO IS |
| THIS DATE ON WHICH WWII ENDED IN EUROPE IN 1945 IS A LEGAL HOLIDAY IN FRANCE | **$1000** | WHAT IS |

# DOUBLE JEOPARDY!

## CELEBRATIONS

$200    **WHAT IS A SANDWICH?**    $200

$400    **WHO IS ROBERT E. LEE?**    $400

$600    **WHAT IS APRIL 16?**    $600

$800    **WHO IS NOAH WEBSTER?**    $800

$1000    **WHAT IS MAY 8?**    $1000

# DOUBLE JEOPARDY!

## "HARD" & "EASY" MOVIES

| Clue | Value | Response |
|---|---|---|
| I'M AWFULLY FONDA HOPPER IN THIS 1969 CLASSIC | $200 | WHAT IS |
| 1964 FILM THAT BROUGHT US A DAY IN THE LIFE OF THE FAB FOUR | $400 | WHAT IS |
| IN THIS FILM THAT LAUNCHED A SERIES, BRUCE WILLIS BATTLES BADDIES IN AN OFFICE TOWER | $600 | WHAT IS |
| BOGART'S LAST FILM, IT WAS BOUT WHAT GOES DOWN IN THE WORLD OF PRIZEFIGHTING | $800 | WHAT IS |
| NEW ORLEANS DETECTIVE DENNIS QUAID CROSSES SWORDS WITH & FALLS FOR D.A. ELLEN BARKIN IN IT | $1000 | WHAT IS |

# DOUBLE JEOPARDY!

## "HARD" & "EASY" MOVIES

$200 — WHAT IS "EASY RIDER"? — $200

$400 — WHAT IS "A HARD DAY'S NIGHT"? — $400

$600 — WHAT IS "DIE HARD"? — $600

$800 — WHAT IS "THE HARDER THEY FALL"? — $800

$1000 — WHAT IS "THE BIG EASY"? — $1000

# DOUBLE JEOPARDY!

## ASSASSINATIONS

| | | |
|---|---|---|
| THIS U.S. PRESIDENT DIED OF A GUNSHOT WOUND IN SEPTEMBER 1881 | **$200** | WHO IS |
| EXECUTED IN 1918, THIS CZAR HAS SINCE BEEN MADE A SAINT BY THE RUSSIAN ORTHODOX CHURCH ABROAD | **$400** | WHO IS |
| U.S. FLAGS FLEW AT HALF STAFF AFTER THIS ISRAELI PRIME MINISTER WAS SLAIN IN 1995 | **$600** | WHO IS |
| 1980s VICTIMS OF BOMBS IN THIS CITY INCLUDED PRESIDENT-ELECT BASHIR GEMAYEL & HUNDREDS OF U.S. MARINES | **$800** | WHAT IS |
| A PRAETORIAN GUARD HAD ENOUGH OF THIS INSANE ROMAN EMPEROR & MURDERED HIM IN 41 A.D. | **$1000** | WHO IS |

# DOUBLE JEOPARDY!

## ASSASSINATIONS

| | | |
|---|---|---|
| **$200** | WHO IS JAMES A. GARFIELD? | **$200** |
| **$400** | WHO IS NICHOLAS II? | **$400** |
| **$600** | WHO IS YITZHAK RABIN? | **$600** |
| **$800** | WHAT IS BEIRUT? | **$800** |
| **$1000** | WHO IS CALIGULA? | **$1000** |

# DOUBLE JEOPARDY!

## 12-LETTER WORDS

| | | |
|---|---|---|
| BRITANNICA OR WORLD BOOK, FOR EXAMPLE | **$200** | WHAT IS |
| IT'S A DOCTOR WHOSE SPECIALTY IS OPERATING ON THE BRAIN & SPINAL CORD | **$400** | WHAT IS |
| IN BOXING, IT'S THE WEIGHT CLASS BETWEEN LIGHTWEIGHT & MIDDLEWEIGHT | **$600** | WHAT IS |
| HOW JIM LANGE USED TO REFER TO A FEMALE CONTESTANT ON TV'S "THE DATING GAME" | **$800** | WHAT IS |
| FROM THE LATIN FOR "TO WALK", IT'S ANOTHER TERM FOR A BABY BUGGY, ESPECIALLY IN BRITAIN | **$1000** | WHAT IS |

# DOUBLE JEOPARDY!

## 12-LETTER WORDS

**$200** | WHAT IS ENCYCLOPEDIA? | **$200**

**$400** | WHAT IS NEUROSURGEON? | **$400**

**$600** | WHAT IS WELTERWEIGHT? | **$600**

**$800** | WHAT IS BACHELORETTE? | **$800**

**$1000** | WHAT IS PERAMBULATOR? | **$1000**

# FINAL JEOPARDY!

## LATIN PHRASES

IT CAN REFER TO THE HOST USED IN THE EUCHARIST, OR A CITY SOUTHWEST OF HOUSTON

WHAT IS

# FINAL JEOPARDY!

## LATIN PHRASES

WHAT IS CORPUS CHRISTI?

# JEOPARDY!

## AROUND THE WORLD

| | | |
|---|---|---|
| IT WASN'T UNTIL 1954, THE YEAR AFTER IT WAS FIRST SCALED, THAT A SURVEY SET IT AT 29,028 FEET | $100 | WHAT IS |
| SMALL SHIPS CAN TRAVEL FROM THIS RIVER'S MOUTH 2,300 MILES UPSTREAM TO IQUITOS, PERU | $200 | WHAT IS |
| IT'S 8 STORIES HIGH, CYLINDRICAL IN SHAPE & ABOUT 14 FEET OFF THE PERPENDICULAR | $300 | WHAT IS |
| ANYTHING BUT BORING ARE THE NORTHERN LIGHTS, ALSO KNOWN BY THIS LATIN NAME | $400 | WHAT IS |
| THIS NATURAL WONDER EXTENDS 1,250 MILES OFF THE NORTHEASTERN COAST OF AUSTRALIA | $500 | WHAT IS |

# JEOPARDY!

## AROUND THE WORLD

$100 | WHAT IS MOUNT EVEREST? | $100

$200 | WHAT IS THE AMAZON? | $200

$300 | WHAT IS THE LEANING TOWER OF PISA? | $300

$400 | WHAT IS AURORA BOREALIS? | $400

$500 | WHAT IS THE GREAT BARRIER REEF? | $500

# JEOPARDY!

## QUOTABLE POTENT POTABLES

| | | |
|---|---|---|
| IN GERMANY THESE PARTY ESSENTIALS ARE CALLED "WEIN, WEIB UND GESANG" | **$100** | WHAT ARE |
| IT'S THE COCKTAIL THAT JAMES BOND LIKES "SHAKEN, NOT STIRRED" | **$200** | WHAT IS |
| THIS ACTOR DRAWLED, "SOME WEASEL TOOK THE CORK OUT OF MY LUNCH" | **$300** | WHO IS |
| IN "TOM BROWN'S SCHOOL DAYS" WE READ THAT "LIFE ISN'T ALL" THIS "AND SKITTLES" | **$400** | WHAT IS |
| SAMUEL JOHNSON SAID, "HE WHO ASPIRES TO BE A HERO MUST DRINK" THIS LIQUOR (NOT NECESSARILY COGNAC) | **$500** | WHAT IS |

# JEOPARDY!™

## QUOTABLE POTENT POTABLES

$100    WHAT ARE WINE, WOMEN & SONG?    $100

$200    WHAT IS A (VODKA) MARTINI?    $200

$300    WHO IS W.C. FIELDS?    $300

$400    WHAT IS BEER?    $400

$500    WHAT IS BRANDY?    $500

# JEOPARDY!

## MEN OF LETTERS

| | | |
|---|---|---|
| THIS RECLUSIVE AUTHOR'S INITIALS STAND FOR JEROME DAVID | **$100** | WHO IS |
| HIS INITIALS STAND FOR EDWARD ESTLIN— OR SHOULD IT BE edward estlin | **$200** | WHO IS |
| DAVID HERBERT WERE THE GIVEN NAMES OF THIS COAL MINER'S SON | **$300** | WHO IS |
| YOU'D USE YOUR INITIALS TOO IF YOUR NAME WAS WYSTAN HUGH, LIKE THIS POET'S | **$400** | WHO IS |
| THE WORK OF THIS MAN CHRISTENED JOHN RONALD REUEL CAN BE HOBBIT FORMING | **$500** | WHO IS |

# JEOPARDY!™

## MEN OF LETTERS

$100 — WHO IS J.D. SALINGER? — $100

$200 — WHO IS e.e. cummings? — $200

$300 — WHO IS D.H. LAWRENCE? — $300

$400 — WHO IS W.H. AUDEN? — $400

$500 — WHO IS J.R.R. TOLKIEN? — $500

# JEOPARDY!

## AFLOAT

| | | |
|---|---|---|
| IF YOU OFTEN CONFUSE LEFT & RIGHT, YOU'LL PROBABLY CONFUSE PORT & THIS | **$100** | WHAT IS |
| SOMEONE HAS TO SWAB THESE, THE EQUIVALENT OF FLOORS, INCLUDING THE POOP & ORLOP | **$200** | WHAT ARE |
| TO "WEIGH" THIS ISN'T TO FIND OUT HOW HEAVY IT IS, BUT TO RAISE IT SO THE SHIP CAN GET UNDER WAY | **$300** | WHAT IS |
| THE AFT PART OF A BOAT, OR AN ADJECTIVE FOR AN ANGRY LOOK | **$400** | WHAT IS |
| IN ANCIENT TIMES IT WAS A VESSEL PROPELLED BY SERVILE OARSMEN; TODAY IT'S A VESSEL'S KITCHEN | **$500** | WHAT IS |

# JEOPARDY!

## AFLOAT

$100 — WHAT IS STARBOARD? — $100

$200 — WHAT ARE DECKS? — $200

$300 — WHAT IS AN ANCHOR? — $300

$400 — WHAT IS STERN? — $400

$500 — WHAT IS THE GALLEY? — $500

# JEOPARDY!™

## TV ON TV

| | | |
|---|---|---|
| "F.Y.I." WAS THE FICTIONAL NEWS SHOW ON THIS SITCOM | **$100** | WHAT IS |
| THIS "SIMPSONS" TV CLOWN HAS WORKED WITH SIDESHOW BOB, SIDESHOW MEL & SIDESHOW LUKE PERRY | **$200** | WHO IS |
| IT'S THE NAME OF THE HOME IMPROVEMENT SHOW FEATURED ON "HOME IMPROVEMENT" | **$300** | WHAT IS |
| HE PLAYED TALK SHOW HOST LARRY SANDERS ON HBO's "THE LARRY SANDERS SHOW" | **$400** | WHO IS |
| SHOW FEATURING PETER KRAUSE, JOSH CHARLES & FELICITY HUFFMAN AS EMPLOYEES OF THE CSC NETWORK | **$500** | WHAT IS |

# JEOPARDY!

## TV ON TV

**$100** WHAT IS "MURPHY BROWN"? **$100**

**$200** WHO IS KRUSTY (THE CLOWN)? (ACCEPT: HERSHEL KRUSTOFSKY) **$200**

**$300** WHAT IS "TOOL TIME"? **$300**

**$400** WHO IS GARRY SHANDLING? **$400**

**$500** WHAT IS "SPORTS NIGHT"? **$500**

# JEOPARDY!™

## FAMOUS BEARDS

| | | |
|---|---|---|
| ACCORDING TO CLEMENT CLARKE MOORE, "THE BEARD ON HIS CHIN WAS AS WHITE AS THE SNOW" | $100 | WHO IS |
| IN THE 1850s HE EXHIBITED MADAME JOSEPHINE FORTUNE CLOFULLIA AS THE "BEARDED LADY FROM SWITZERLAND" | $200 | WHO IS |
| END-OF-THE- ALPHABET BAND WITH DRUMMER FRANK BEARD AS THE ONLY BEARDLESS MEMBER | $300 | WHAT IS |
| GRACE BEDELL, AGE 11, THOUGHT THIS MAN WOULD WIN AN ELECTION BY MORE THAN A HAIR IF HE GREW WHISKERS; HE AGREED | $400 | WHO IS |
| FOR THIS AUSTRIAN PSYCHOANALYST, SOMETIMES A BEARD WAS JUST A BEARD | $500 | WHO IS |

# JEOPARDY!

## FAMOUS BEARDS

**$100** — WHO IS ST. NICHOLAS? (ACCEPT: ST. NICK, SANTA CLAUS) — **$100**

**$200** — WHO IS P(HINEAS) T(AYLOR) BARNUM? — **$200**

**$300** — WHAT IS ZZ TOP? — **$300**

**$400** — WHO IS ABRAHAM LINCOLN? — **$400**

**$500** — WHO IS SIGMUND FREUD? — **$500**

298

# DOUBLE JEOPARDY!

## WORLD LEADERS

| | | |
|---|---|---|
| IN NOVEMBER 1999 CHERIE, THE WIFE OF THIS BRITISH PRIME MINISTER, ANNOUNCED SHE WAS PREGNANT | **$200** | WHO IS |
| IN 1967 MUDA HASSANAL BOLKIAH BECAME THE INSANELY WEALTHY SULTAN OF THIS COUNTRY | **$400** | WHAT IS |
| HELMUT KOHL PASSED THIS MAN'S RECORD AS THE LONGEST-SERVING CHANCELLOR OF POST-WWII GERMANY | **$600** | WHO IS |
| PRESIDENTS OF THIS COUNTRY SINCE ITS 1970s REVOLUTION INCLUDE RAFSANJANI & KHATAMI | **$800** | WHAT IS |
| THIS MAN OF JAPANESE DESCENT GAINED THE PRESIDENCY OF PERU IN 1990 | **$1000** | WHO IS |

# DOUBLE JEOPARDY!

## WORLD LEADERS

| | | |
|---|---|---|
| **$200** | WHO IS TONY BLAIR? | **$200** |
| **$400** | WHAT IS BRUNEI? | **$400** |
| **$600** | WHO IS KONRAD ADENAUER? | **$600** |
| **$800** | WHAT IS IRAN? | **$800** |
| **$1000** | WHO IS ALBERTO KENYO FUJIMORI? | **$1000** |

# DOUBLE JEOPARDY!

## ASTRONOMY

| | | |
|---|---|---|
| THE CRAB NEBULA, FIRST OBSERVED IN 1054 A.D., CAN BE FOUND IN THIS CONSTELLATION, & THAT'S NO BULL | **$200** | WHAT IS |
| DUE TO ITS COILED ARMS, THE MILKY WAY IS CLASSIFIED AS THIS TYPE OF GALAXY, ALSO THE NAME OF A TYPE OF STAIRCASE | **$400** | WHAT IS |
| UNTIL 1974 THE 200-INCH HALE TELESCOPE ON THIS CALIFORNIA MOUNTAIN WAS THE WORLD'S LARGEST REFLECTOR | **$600** | WHAT IS |
| THIS ITALIAN SPENT HIS LAST 8 YEARS UNDER HOUSE ARREST FOR TEACHING...SHH! THE EARTH GOES AROUND THE SUN! | **$800** | WHO IS |
| BY THE TIME THIS FLOW OF GASES FROM THE SUN REACHES EARTH, ITS SPEED MAY BE 1-2 MILLION MPH | **$1000** | WHAT IS |

# DOUBLE JEOPARDY!

## ASTRONOMY

$200  —  WHAT IS TAURUS?  —  $200

$400  —  WHAT IS A SPIRAL GALAXY?  —  $400

$600  —  WHAT IS MOUNT PALOMAR?  —  $600

$800  —  WHO IS GALILEO (GALILEI)?  —  $800

$1000  —  WHAT IS THE SOLAR WIND?  —  $1000

302

# DOUBLE JEOPARDY!

## MOVIE STARS

| Clue | Value | Response |
|------|-------|----------|
| YOU MAY CALL HIM ROCKY OR RAMBO, BUT HIS FRIENDS CALL HIM SLY | **$200** | WHO IS |
| ELSA LANCHESTER PLAYED THIS TITLE "BRIDE" WHO HAD THE WORST BAD HAIR DAY OF ALL TIME | **$400** | WHO IS |
| THIS STAR OF "GIRL, INTERRUPTED" IS THE GODDAUGHTER OF '60s GURU DR. TIMOTHY LEARY | **$600** | WHO IS |
| JAMIE LEE CURTIS WASN'T BORN YET WHEN THESE ACTORS, HER PARENTS, CO-STARRED IN "HOUDINI" IN 1953 | **$800** | WHO ARE |
| HER FIERY PERFORMANCE AS NICK NOLTE'S DAUGHTER IN "CAPE FEAR" EARNED HER AN OSCAR NOMINATION | **$1000** | WHO IS |

# DOUBLE JEOPARDY!

## MOVIE STARS

$200  WHO IS SYLVESTER STALLONE?  $200

$400  WHO IS THE BRIDE OF FRANKENSTEIN?  $400

$600  WHO IS WINONA RYDER?  $600

$800  WHO ARE TONY CURTIS & JANET LEIGH?  $800

$1000  WHO IS JULIETTE LEWIS?  $1000

# DOUBLE JEOPARDY!

## HOT STUFF

| | | |
|---|---|---|
| BLACKSMITHS WERE THE ORIGINAL OPPORTUNISTS WHO "STRUCK WHILE" THIS WAS HOT | **$200** | WHAT IS |
| 15 SECONDS AT 160 DEGREES F. KILLS THIS BACTERIUM THAT IN 1997 CAUSED THE USA's BIGGEST BEEF RECALL | **$400** | WHAT IS |
| A SECOND AFTER THIS HYPOTHESIZED EXPLOSION, THE TEMPERATURE WAS 10 BILLION DEGREES KELVIN | **$600** | WHAT IS |
| PLAIN OLD WATER IS A COMMON COOLANT FOR THIS PART OF A NUCLEAR REACTOR YOU MIGHT CALL THE "FISSION HOLE" | **$800** | WHAT IS |
| FORECASTS ON THIS PLANET CALL FOR HIGHS OF 800 DEGREES F. & BLACK SKIES DUE TO LACK OF SIGNIFI-CANT ATMOSPHERE | **$1000** | WHAT IS |

# DOUBLE JEOPARDY!

## HOT STUFF

**$200** — WHAT IS THE IRON? — **$200**

**$400** — WHAT IS E. COLI (0157.H7)? (ACCEPT: ESCHERICHIA) — **$400**

**$600** — WHAT IS THE BIG BANG? — **$600**

**$800** — WHAT IS THE CORE? — **$800**

**$1000** — WHAT IS MERCURY? — **$1000**

# DOUBLE JEOPARDY!

## A CAPITAL IDEA

| | | |
|---|---|---|
| THIS CITY'S PEACE TOWER HOUSES A MEMORIAL CHAMBER COMMEMORATING CANADA'S WAR DEAD | **$200** | WHAT IS |
| THE BEAR IS THE HERALDIC SYMBOL OF THIS SWISS CAPITAL | **$400** | WHAT IS |
| THIS COUNTRY'S CAPITAL, AMMAN, LIES A BIT NORTHEAST OF THE DEAD SEA | **$600** | WHAT IS |
| THE GREEKS CALL CYPRUS' CAPITAL LEVKOSIA; THE TURKS CALL IT LEFKOSA; WE CALL IT THIS | **$800** | WHAT IS |
| ST. STEPHEN LENT A HAND, HIS MUMMIFIED RIGHT HAND, TO ST. STEPHEN'S BASILICA IN THIS CAPITAL | **$1000** | WHAT IS |

# DOUBLE JEOPARDY!

## A CAPITAL IDEA

$200    WHAT IS OTTAWA?    $200

$400    WHAT IS BERN?    $400

$600    WHAT IS JORDAN?    $600

$800    WHAT IS NICOSIA?    $800

$1000    WHAT IS BUDAPEST?    $1000

# DOUBLE JEOPARDY!

## "BOO"!

| Clue | Value | Response |
|------|-------|----------|
| IT'S A FOLLOW-UP DOSE OF A VACCINE; ONE SHOULD BE GIVEN AT AGE 2 & ANOTHER BEFORE ENTERING SCHOOL | $200 | WHAT IS |
| COUNT CHOCULA'S GHOSTLY COMPANION IN THE CEREAL WORLD | $400 | WHO IS |
| JEM & SCOUT'S CREEPY BUT HELPFUL NEIGHBOR IN "TO KILL A MOCKINGBIRD" | $600 | WHO IS |
| NICKNAME OF EYE-CATCHING P-FUNK BASSIST WILLIAM COLLINS | $800 | WHAT IS |
| THIS TYPE OF ALGEBRA USES "AND", "OR" & "NOT" AS OPERATORS THAT RESTRICT SEARCHES ON THE INTERNET | $1000 | WHAT IS |

# DOUBLE JEOPARDY!

## "BOO"!

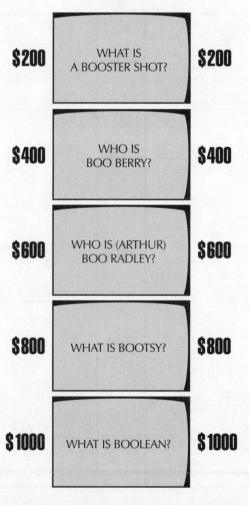

**$200**   WHAT IS A BOOSTER SHOT?   **$200**

**$400**   WHO IS BOO BERRY?   **$400**

**$600**   WHO IS (ARTHUR) BOO RADLEY?   **$600**

**$800**   WHAT IS BOOTSY?   **$800**

**$1000**   WHAT IS BOOLEAN?   **$1000**

# FINAL JEOPARDY!

## RETAIL

FRUSTRATED BY
DEPARTMENT STORES,
DONALD FISHER FOUNDED
THIS CHAIN IN 1969 AS A
RECORD & JEANS STORE

WHAT IS

# FINAL JEOPARDY!

## RETAIL

WHAT IS THE GAP (, INC.)?